T0311209

Nietzsche's Negative Ecologies

THE TOWNSEND PAPERS IN THE HUMANITIES *No. 1*

Nietzsche's Negative Ecologies

Malcolm Bull
Anthony J. Cascardi
T.J. Clark

Published by
The Townsend Center for the Humanities
University of California | Berkeley

Distributed by
Fordham University Press
New York | 2009

Copyright ©2009 The Regents of the University of California

Library of Congress Control Number 2009927426

ISBN 978-0-9823294-0-5

"Where Is the Anti-Nietzsche" was originally published in
New Left Review 3 (May–June 2000). Used by permission.

Inquiries concerning proposals for the Townsend Papers in the Humanities
from Berkeley faculty and Townsend Center affiliates should be addressed to
The Townsend Papers, 220 Stephens Hall, UC Berkeley, Berkeley, CA 94720-
2340, or by email to townsend_papers@lists.berkeley.edu

Design and typesetting: Kajun Graphics

Manufactured in the United States of America

Table of Contents

Anthony J. Cascardi

"Slow Reading": A Preface to Nietzsche

"Festina lente" (Make haste slowly)
—Erasmus/Aldus

AMONG PHILOSOPHICAL WRITERS, or thinkers of any kind, there are few whose impact could rival that of Friedrich Nietzsche on the course of the humanities during the last several decades. Nietzsche is nearly everywhere, or so it seems—to the point that it is not at all unreasonable to ask "Where Is the Anti-Nietzsche?" as does Malcolm Bull in these pages. This is a puzzling state of affairs. Nietzsche hardly saw himself as the founder of a school, and even the idea of "influence" seems anomalous in light of a body of work that contains very little in the way of a fixed set of views. An orthodoxy seems nonetheless to have emerged from the work of the most unorthodox of thinkers.

The Nietzsche who has become *de rigueur* is a figure more often invoked than cited, and more often cited than read. When read, Nietzsche's texts are typically mined for their philosophical views. (A number of studies on Nietzsche and literature published beginning in the 1980s seem to have done little to change this state of affairs.)[1] This is further puzzling, since Nietzsche himself spoke explicitly about how his works ought to be approached.

Some of the remarks in question occur at the conclusion of the preface to *Daybreak* (*Morgenröthe*). This is where Nietzsche famously demands to be read *slowly*, explaining that slow reading may prove especially difficult in an age of haste and hard work: "[I]t is more necessary than ever today…in the midst of an age of 'work,' that is to say, of hurry, of indecent and perspiring haste, which wants to 'get everything done' at once, including every old or new book:—this art does not so easily get anything done, it teaches us to read *well*, that is to say, to read slowly, deeply, looking cautiously before and aft, with reservations, with doors left open, with delicate eyes and fingers.'"[2] It is far from given that the kind of reading Nietzsche has in mind can ever fully be accomplished. After all, Nietzsche himself recognized that he was demanding "perfect readers and philologists." "*Learn* to read me well," he says; but reading Nietzsche in the way he demands requires a skill we may never be able to master to perfection.

What is the "slow reading" Nietzsche imagines? Literary criticism has long known the practice of something called "close reading." Its protocols are familiar to anyone trained in literary studies during the decades following the Second World War. Even as literature later opened itself to various forms of "theory" and came to recognize the workings of history within the text, the ideals of close reading remained very much intact. To slow down enough to devote close attention to what is said (and to how it is said), to attend to the nuances of voice and form, to listen, and to give oneself over to the qualities that are particular to a given work, rather than to proceed with "perspiring haste" in order to "get everything done" with a text, requires equal measures of discipline and patience. To read in this way is a practice and not a science, and least of all a science of knowledge. It is, moreover, a practice that demands a posture of respect vis-à-vis the text. By contrast, the search for assertions that can be put to immediate use, including immediate political use, would seem to require reading with undue haste.

To read closely requires that one allow oneself to be guided by the text, that one agree to follow its lead, rather than to lead it. Is this what slow reading would also require? Perhaps. The practices do share one common set of roots. Nietzsche was himself trained as a philologist and was appointed professor of Greek philology at the University of Basel in 1869, three years before his first book (*The Birth of Tragedy*) appeared. But he advocates "slow reading" as a way of explaining the manner in which one particular book, *Daybreak*, was fashioned; from that account he extrapolates an idea about how a "perfect reader" might approach his work. Slow reading is meant to mirror Nietzsche's writing and ultimately to mirror Nietzsche himself. Like many of Nietzsche's works, and especially those of the period between 1878 and 1882, *Daybreak* was fashioned from a series of notes. The book consists of polished and edited versions of passages that Nietzsche wrote down on walks in Riva, Venice, Marienbad, and Genoa.[3] In a very late passage ("Digression") he remarks that *Daybreak* was designed for dipping into, not for reading straight through; it requires errant reading: "[A] book such as this is not for reading straight through or reading aloud but for dipping into, especially when out walking or on a journey; you must be able to stick your head into it and out of it again and again and discover nothing familiar around you."[4] The text is arranged as a series of fragments, each of which is announced by a heading; but these headings (for example, "Empathy," "Night and music," "Do not renounce") hardly conform to a single paradigm.

To whom does Nietzsche address himself in these remarks? Is it the "patient friends" (*meine geduldigen Freunde*) he mentions in section 2 of the preface? Perhaps, except that this remark may be taken simply as acknowledging the fact that he has been slow to publish the book. More revealing is Nietzsche's admission that no reader may be able to follow him, insofar as he is a "subterranean [*unterirdisch*] man" who rejects disciples even as he asks to be read slowly. Even while soliciting the reader he poses as a solitary soul. "I shall now tell you what I was after down there," Nietzsche says of his subsurface soundings; "[but] do not think for a moment that I intend to invite you to the same hazardous enterprise! Or even only to the same solitude! For he who proceeds on his own path in this fashion encounters no one: that is inherent in 'proceeding in one's own path.'"[5] One is reminded of the fact that *Thus Spoke Zarathustra* was written to be "A Book for Everyone and No One."

How then to read Nietzsche "slowly" while also proceeding on one's own path? The answer may of course depend on the specific text in question. Nietzsche's corpus comprises at least three different types of texts, each one of which poses a distinct set of reading challenges. All of them together place substantial obstacles in the way of anyone who would hope to hasten them toward an "authoritative" set of views. (I say this in full view of the fact that Nietzsche often speaks in a voice that sounds remarkably authoritative—all too authoritative, one might say.) *Daybreak* exemplifies the works that Nietzsche crafted in journal form, works that originated as notes or thought-experiments, written in the first instance for Nietzsche himself. The fragments that comprise *The Will to Power* are perhaps the preeminent example of this type of work. It is often said that *Will to Power* is simply an assemblage of remarks and not a book in the conventional sense, but the more important fact is that these remarks were written and revised, in the first instance and maybe in the last, for Nietzsche's own philosophical ear. He writes and listens to the sound of what he says, then thinks, reacts, revises, and writes more. The headings of *Daybreak* and *Will to Power* are rather like prompts or instigations, not a series of well-formed categories or summaries of any particular line of thought. How to read anything that Nietzsche says in these fragments, if not in a correspondingly fragmentary way? In the preface to *Daybreak* (which was written, like nearly all prefaces, after the fact), Nietzsche asks us to wander without immediate intent or purpose. Yet no reader, it seems, will be able to absorb what these texts seem to demand—reading slowly and errantly—and still have these fragments "make sense."

Not all of Nietzsche's works are of this sort. There are essays, such as the early *Birth of Tragedy*, that seem to articulate their views in a more or less conventional form. So too the short polemical pieces published in *Untimely Meditations*, including "Schopenhauer as Educator," "The Uses and Abuses of History for Life," and "David Strauss, the Confessor and the Writer." It would seem tempting to take *Birth of Tragedy* as a straightforward account of the entanglement of the "Dionysian" and "Apollonian" impulses and of their subsequent suppression by philosophy. But Nietzsche's immense admiration for Richard Wagner in *Birth of Tragedy* fuels an enthusiasm that leads him well beyond analysis. Indeed, it would not be unfair to say that Nietzsche wrote *Birth of Tragedy* under a Wagnerian "spell." Nietzsche himself recognized this much in his subsequent repudiation of the work. The relationship between Apollonian and Dionysian elements as formulated in *Birth of Tragedy* is on one level a reflection of the interplay between force and form. But the book was also the starting point of a titanic struggle with Wagner, and, in order to overcome the power of Wagner's presence over the work, Nietzsche ultimately found himself needing to reject it wholesale ("Nietzsche Contra Wagner"). The experience taught Nietzsche something powerful about the dynamics of influence; it was key to the development of his own stance as a writer who reserves the highest place among the circle of his readers for truly creative spirits.

The essays published right after *Birth of Tragedy* already begin to explore new rhetorical registers. In *Untimely Meditations* there is ironic praise for Schopenhauer's "cheerfulness," which Nietzsche likens to Montaigne's. By contrast, the essay on David Strauss is peppered with satire and criticism, sometimes to the point of insult and abuse; and there are frequent remarks on the philistinism of the Germans in "On the Use and Abuse of History for Life." No doubt Nietzsche had good reason to denounce much of what he saw around him. But the aggressive tone of these remarks serves as more than a severe indictment of his targets: the tone borders on the indecorous, and Nietzsche knew that the book was likely to seem unwelcome and out of joint with the times ("untimely"). His own sense of torment provides one justification for the book's tone. But this is a torment he scarcely wished to relinquish. *Untimely Meditations* bears the marks of a writer who has learned to listen to himself, and who seems to relish the sound of his own voice as it parries and thrusts. Wary of the dangers of auto-affection, the essays stage a verbal drama of enticement and recoil that is especially hazardous to any reader who might try to move through them too fast.

> I have striven to depict a feeling by which I am constantly
> tormented; I revenge myself upon it by handing it over to the
> public. Perhaps this depiction will inspire someone or other to
> tell me that he too knows this feeling but that I have felt it in
> its pure and elemental state and have certainly not expressed
> it with the assurance that comes from mature experience.
> Someone, I say, may perhaps do so: most people, however,
> will tell me that this feeling is altogether perverse, unnatural,
> detestable and wholly impermissible, and that by feeling it I
> have shown myself unworthy of the mighty historical move-
> ment which, as is well known, has been in evidence among the
> Germans particularly for the past two generations.[6]

We who imagine ourselves to be good readers (that is, slow readers, or at least close readers) can easily be tempted to identify with Nietzsche against the "Germans" of his age. But whoever would identify with Nietzsche in such a way will inevitably run afoul of a rhetoric that ends by attacking anyone who would not become an artist-creator in his or her own right: "When the great thinker despises mankind, he despises its laziness: for it is on account of their laziness…The man who does not wish to belong to the mass needs only to cease taking himself easily; let him follow his con-science, which calls to him: 'Be your self! All you are now doing, thinking, desiring, is not you yourself.'"[7]

This is not so much a rhetoric of authenticity or rugged individualism as it is a form of goading. It blossoms into flowers of cheer and vitriol in the fragments that comprise *Will to Power*. Some offer straightforward indictments: "*The patrons of virtue*: Avarice, lust to rule, laziness, simplicity, fear: all have an interest in the cause of virtue: that is why it stands so firm"; "The psychological error out of which the antithetical concepts 'moral' and 'immoral' arose is: 'selfless,' 'unegoistic,' 'self-denying'—all unreal, imaginary."[8] Examples could be multiplied at length. Together with the claims of *Beyond Good and Evil* and *The Genealogy of Morals* there is enough in these works to allow for a formulation of Nietzsche's "teaching" on morality and nihilism. The heart of that teaching would lie in Nietzsche's assertions that morality stands in the way of existence and was invented mainly as an antidote against nihilism.[9] "Morality" builds its faith upon a fictitious view of the world ("We have measured the value of the world according to categories that refer to a purely fictitious world").[10] Nietzsche, by contrast speaks the truth.

But how? Who except a seer would claim to have rent the fiction of the world, and how can a seer communicate what he knows? This is an especially great challenge given the thoroughness of Nietzsche's suspicion of the many alliances, implicit or explicit, between virtue and the fantasy of God's voice ("One needed God as an unconditional sanction, with no court of appeal, as a 'categorical imperative'—: or, if one believed in the authority of reason, one needed a metaphysics of unity, by virtue of which this was logical"). But there is more: if we do relinquish God, Nietzsche answers that what we are bound to hear speak in us is the voice of the herd that wants to be master ("*the herd instinct speaks*. It wants to be master").[11]

All the works that deal with nihilism struggle with the question of voice: who speaks, to and for whom, and how? Not surprisingly, perhaps, the voice of *Will to Power* edges toward extremes even as it rails against ignorance and excess. One fragment, written in 1887 and revised the following year, reads: "Petty people's morality as the measure of things: this is the most disgusting degeneration culture has yet exhibited. And this kind of ideal still hanging over mankind as 'God'!!"[12] A certain extremism is no doubt fitting for a project of unmasking that aims to achieve radical results. And yet some of what strikes us as potentially outrageous and offensive is uttered with absolute calm. There may be little need to inject hyperbole into the statements about "rank" in relation to "power," which are outrageous enough on their own: "What determines rank, sets off rank, is only quanta of power, and nothing else."[13] But there are political and psychological consequences that follow from opposition to what Nietzsche here says: to believe that there are no differences in power would be to identify with the herd; to posit that everyone can be equally reintegrated into some "whole" undermines the very basis of human striving. Moreover, in Nietzsche's views the herd "hates those who detach themselves—it turns the hatred of all individuals against them."[14] No doubt Nietzsche himself felt this detachment in good measure and cultivated it as well.

The Will to Power does at one point offer its own solution to the problem of communication. It is not one that an ordinary writer can easily embrace. "Compared with music," Nietzsche writes, "all communication by words is shameless; words dilute and brutalize; words depersonalize; words make the uncommon common."[15] But we do not know which music (except that it will not be Wagner), and there is no way of telling who will know how to listen.

What we do know is that the appropriation of Nietzsche by intellectuals intending to work in the service of radical democracy has also put those intellectuals on the spot. It is not uncommon to find oneself applauding Nietzsche's critique of morality while having to pick through the minefield of his remarks, approving what he might say about metaphysics, for example, while carefully denouncing what he says on such topics as women and rank ordering. Nietzsche's critique of power has been appropriated in a more seamless and less dangerous form, via Foucault. Some have posited that Nietzsche forces us to confront the undemocratic impulses that make democracy possible (as opposed to just necessary).[16] Nietzsche may still seem compelling to those groups that have felt themselves betrayed by what Slavoj Žiž ek calls the modern "liberal-egalitarian framework of human rights"[17]—not least because the institutions charged with making good on the integrative promises of democracy have continued to mask democracy's incomplete inclusion of, for example, women, gays, and people of color. But the "Nietzschean" alternative to democracy seems at least as problematic as this version of democracy itself— if, that is, we regard Nietzsche as offering a theoretical stance or set of ethical imperatives that can be put to political use. Framed in those terms, there is no reasonable way in which Nietzsche can be wrestled into line with democratic views nor any obvious way in which democracy can be bent to a Nietzschean stance.

The third type of work I have in mind, epitomized by *Thus Spoke Zarathustra*, shifts this question to the relations between poetry and democracy. *Zarathustra* is neither a compilation of fragments nor an essay, but a poetic rhapsody. (To speak in musical terms, one might describe it as a "fantasia.") It is a composition in which Nietzsche speaks not in wordless tones but through metaphors and images, in poetic and prophetic tones, by means of an alter ego. It requires reading on at least two levels at once. On one level, *Zarathustra* says nothing less than the "truth": Zarathustra, the character at least, says what he means and means what he says. ("My brothers in war! I love you from the very heart....So let me tell you the truth!").[18] But as poet and as prophet Zarathustra also speaks indirectly, in figures and tropes whose meanings lie concealed. This is especially the case in part 3 of the book, where the imagery grows uncommonly thick and dense. As a Greek philologist, Nietzsche would have been well aware of the ancient narrative strategy that requires concealment, or intentional secrecy, as a condition of the truth.[19] One is reminded of what the dwarf says in "Of the Vision and the Riddle": "'Everything straight lies... All truth is crooked.'"[20] But what does Nietzsche's poetic way of speaking mean for attempts to enlist him in the project of "radical" cultural and political critique? Can the result possibly be democratic? Can any poetry be democratic?

We do of course know examples of democratic poetry, at least in the American context, ranging from Whitman's *Leaves of Grass* to Langston Hughes's National Poetry Project. Their respective aims were to speak for the multitudes (Whitman) and to put the voice of poetry back in the mouths of the people (Hughes). But the rhetorical principles that underlie civic discourse in democratic societies—the free and equal exchange of ideas, above all—seem to stand opposed to anything like the poetry that speaks to the few; there is scarcely room in modern democracy for the poets of the *trobar clus* or for hieratic speech. The victory of the *demos* was achieved in a secular context, as a victory of the many over the few. Reflecting on Malcolm Bull's essays, one might well recognize how reading "like a loser" can help salvage Nietzsche for the sake of a new moral ecology. But the further question is what kind of poetry can it salvage for democracy? And this is in the end what radical intellectuals would need to answer in order to do much with Nietzsche's political views.

Let us pursue this question one further step. The implicit politics of *Zarathustra* is a new Athenian universalism. It seeks to overcome all the former failed attempts to fuse the ideals of Athens and Jerusalem into one. We know that the result will be unrecognizable as a form of modern democracy and will likewise not resemble any form of democracy that conforms to the visions of radical intellectuals. Indeed, the Nietzsche that seems to be so desired by contemporary intellectuals is by his own admission homeless in modern Europe.[21] He may nonetheless provide a source of significant *resistance* for modern Europeans and their American fellow-travelers. As Laurence Lampert has argued, "[Nietzsche] remains who he is despite attempts by friends and enemies alike to make him into something he is not."[22] But Nietzsche often portrayed himself as something he was not; his masks were a condition of speaking the truth. He did not present himself as a political thinker, and as a "philosopher" he fashioned himself as a poet, that is, as someone who speaks in a series of voices, in figures and in tones that range from the heights of the solemn to comical extremes. Whoever enters a work like *Zarathustra* in a literal frame of mind is bound to be overwhelmed by the text.

We know that it would take a poet or a seer (or a madman) to intone the truth from the mountain heights or the depths of a cave. But Zarathustra's call is for a new order of poetry as much as it is a call for anything else: "I have grown weary of the poets, the old and the new; they all seem to me superficial and shallow seas. They have not thought deeply enough: therefore their feeling—has not plumbed the depths."[23] What we do *not* know is whether Zarathustra has access to a special type of knowledge, or whether he simply claims knowledge that we all might have, just veiled in a special kind of discourse. Suppose for a moment that the latter were true, and that Zarathustra's heightened views—his views from the heights—were in fact a reflection of some basic truths? Suppose, further, that we were to take everything Zarathustra says as true, but not true here, or now. (Zarathustra himself recognizes that "there is something of me that is of to-morrow and of the day-after-tomorrow and of the shall-be.")[24] What then of reading Nietzsche's poetry for democracy's sake? Might we re-imagine the polis along these lines, recognizing that it is not meant for here or now, but for elsewhere, or another time? The result is unlikely to resemble democracy in any form we have known it yet—to which should also be added Nietzsche's cautionary remark that we ought to proceed slowly and not with overhasty zeal.

Endnotes

1 See for example Sara Kofman, *Nietzsche et la Métaphore* (Paris, 1983), Alexander Nehamas, *Nietzsche, Life as Literature* (Cambridge, 1985), and Henry Staten, Nietzsche's Voice (Ithaca, 1990).

2 Friedrich Nietzsche, *Daybreak*, trans. R. J. Hollingdale (Cambridge, 1982), p. 5. (Except where indicated by the abbreviation "p." for "page," references to Nietzsche's works are to section numbers, not page numbers.)

3 See the very helpful introduction by Michael Tanner in ibid.

4 Ibid., p. 191.

5 Ibid., p. 1.

6 Friedrich Nietzsche, "On the Uses and Disadvantages of History for Life," in *Untimely Meditations*, trans. R. J. Hollingdale (Cambridge, 1983), p. 59.

7 Friedrich Nietzsche, "Schopenhauer as Educator," in *Untimely Meditations*, p. 127.

8 Friedrich Nietzsche, *The Will to Power*, trans. Walter Kaufmann and R. J. Hollingdale (New York, 1968), 323, p. 178; 786, p. 413; hereafter WP.

9 See esp. WP, 4 and 6, p. 10.

10 WP, 12B, p. 13.

11 Both passages are from WP, 275, p. 157.

12 WP, 200, p. 117.

13 WP, 854, p. 457.

14 WP, 275, p. 157.

15 WP, 810, p. 428.

16 See for example Wendy Brown, *Politics Out of History* (Princeton, 2001).

17 See Slavoj Žižek, *In Defense of Lost Causes* (London, 2008), p. 102.

18 Friedrich Nietzsche, *Thus Spoke Zarathustra*, trans. R.J. Hollingdale (Harmondsworth, 1969), p. 73.

19 Nietzsche echoes the biblical parable that engages this very tradition of intentional secrecy when he writes, "He who has ears to hear, let him hear," ibid., p. 178. See Frank Kermode, *The Genesis of Secrecy* (Cambridge, 1979). There are, in addition, a series of open secrets in the book, such as the identification in part 4 of Richard Wagner as the sorcerer and of Schopenhauer as the "gloomy prophet."

20 Nietzsche, *Thus Spoke Zarathustra*, p. 176.

21 Friedrich Nietzsche, *The Gay Science*, trans. Walter Kaufmann (New York, 1974), 377.

[22] Ibid., 378–80; Laurence Lampert, *Nietzsche and Modern Times: A Study of Bacon, Descartes, and Nietzsche* (New Haven, 1993), p. 428.

[23] *Zarathustra*, p. 151.

[24] Ibid., p. 150.

Malcolm Bull

Where Is the Anti-Nietzsche?

OPPOSED TO EVERYONE, Nietzsche has met with remarkably little opposition. In fact, his reputation has suffered only one apparent reverse—his enthusiastic adoption by the Nazis. But, save in Germany, Nietzsche's association with the horrors of the Second World War and the Holocaust has served chiefly to stimulate further curiosity. Of course, the monster has had to be tamed, and Nietzsche's thought has been cleverly reconstructed so as perpetually to evade the evils perpetrated in his name. Even those philosophies for which he consistently reserved his most biting contempt—socialism, feminism, and Christianity—have sought to appropriate their tormentor. Almost everybody now claims Nietzsche as one of their own; he has become what he most wanted to be—irresistible.

This situation gives added significance to a number of recent publications in which the authors reverse the standard practice and straightforwardly report what Nietzsche wrote in order to distance themselves from it. Ishay Landa's article, in which he persuasively argues against the idea that Nietzsche was anything other than dismissive of workers' rights, is one example.[1] But it is only the latest in a small flurry of books and articles that take a more critical view of Nietzsche's thought. The anti-Nietzschean turn began in France, where Luc Ferry and Alain Renant's collection, *Pourquoi nous ne sommes pas nietzschéens* (1991), responded to the Nietzsche/Marx/Freud syntheses of the preceding decades with the demand that "We have to stop *interpreting* Nietzsche and start taking him at his word."[2] The contributors emphasized Nietzsche's opposition to truth and rational argument, the disturbing consequences of his inegalitarianism and immoralism, and his influence on reactionary thought. Ferry and Renant were seeking to renew a traditional humanism, but anti-Nietzscheanism can take very different forms. Geoff Waite's cornucopian *Nietzsche's Corps/e* (1996) links the end of Communism and the triumph of Nietzscheanism, and approaches Nietzsche and his body of interpreters from an Althusserian perspective from which Nietzsche emerges as "the revolutionary programmer of late pseudo-leftist, fascoid-liberal culture and technoculture."[3] Claiming that, in that it is now "blasphemy only to blaspheme *Nietzsche*—formerly the great blasphemer—and his community," Waite proceeds to uncover Nietzsche's "esoteric" teachings which aim "to re/produce a viable form of willing human slavery appropriate to post/modern conditions, and with it a small number of (male) geniuses equal only among themselves."[4] Integral to this teaching is what Waite calls the "'hermeneutic' or 'rhetoric of euthanasia': *the process of weeding out.*" Those who cannot withstand the thought of Eternal Recurrence are, Nietzsche claims, unfit for life: "Whosoever will be destroyed with the sentence 'there is no salvation' ought to die. I want wars, in which the vital and courageous drive out the others."[5]

Although Fredrick Appel's succinctly argued *Nietzsche Contra Democracy* (1999) could hardly be more different from *Nietzsche's Corps/e* in style, the argument is similar. Appel complains that as "efforts to draft Nietzsche's thought into the service of radical democracy have multiplied...his patently inegalitarian political project [has been] ignored or summarily dismissed." Far from being a protean thinker whose thought is so multifaceted as to resist any single political interpretation, Nietzsche is committed to "an uncompromising repudiation of both the ethic of benevolence and the notion of the equality of persons in the name of a radically aristocratic commitment to human excellence."[6] Unlike Waite, who suggests that Nietzsche to some degree concealed his political agenda, Appel argues that it pervades every aspect of Nietzsche's later thought. Nietzsche's elitism is not only fundamental to his entire worldview, it is so profound that it leads naturally to the conclusion that "the great majority of men have no right to existence."[7]

Appel draws attention to Nietzsche's political programme not in order to exclude Nietzsche from the political debate but "to invite democracy's friends to face the depth of his challenge head-on with a reasoned and effective defence of democratic ideals."[8] Appel himself gives no indication of what the appropriate defence might be. For Waite, who takes up Bataille's suggestion that "Nietzsche's position is the only one outside of communism," the answer is clear: the only anti-Nietzschean position is a "communist" one, vaguely defined as an assortment of social practices leading to total liberation.[9] However, Waite does not say how or why such a position should be considered preferable. Nietzsche's arguments were explicitly formulated against the practices of social levelling and liberation found within Christianity, liberalism, socialism, and feminism. Pointing out that Nietzsche's thought is incompatible with such projects is, as Appel rightly emphasizes, only the beginning.

But from where should Nietzsche be opposed? Most of his recent critics seek to reaffirm political and philosophical positions that Nietzsche himself repudiated. For them, reestablishing that Nietzsche was an amoral, irrationalist, anti-egalitarian who had no respect for basic human rights suffices as a means of disposing of his arguments. Yet if opposition comes only from within the pre-existing traditions, it will do little to dislodge Nietzsche from the position that he chose for himself—the philosopher of the future who writes "for a species of man that does not yet exist." [10] The self-styled Anti-Christ who placed himself on the last day of Christianity, and at the end of the secular European culture that it had fostered, would not be displeased if his "revaluation of all values" were to be indefinitely rejected by those who continued to adhere to the values he despised. He would live forever as their eschatological nemesis, the limit-philosopher of a modernity that never ends, waiting to be born posthumously on the day after tomorrow. What seems to be missing is any critique of Nietzsche that takes the same retrospective position that Nietzsche adopted with regard to Christianity. Postmodernity has spawned plenty of post-Nietzscheans anxious to appropriate Nietzsche for their own agendas, but there appear to be no post-Nietzschean anti-Nietzscheans, no critics whose response is designed not to prevent us from getting to Nietzsche, but to enable us to get over him.

Reading Nietzsche

THE CHIEF IMPEDIMENT to the development of any form of anti-Nietzscheanism is, as Waite points out, that "most readers basically *trust* him." [11] One reason for this is that Nietzsche gives readers strong incentives to do so. "This book belongs to the very few," he announces in the foreword to *The Anti-Christ*. It belongs only to those who are "honest in intellectual matters to the point of harshness"; who have "Strength which prefers questions for which no one today is sufficiently daring; courage for the *forbidden*":

> These alone are my readers, my rightful readers, my predes-tined readers: what do the rest matter?—The rest are merely mankind.—One must be superior to mankind in force, in *loftiness* of soul—in contempt...[12]

Through the act of reading, Nietzsche flatteringly offers identifica-tion with the masters to anyone, but not to everyone. Identification with the masters means imaginative liberation from all the social, moral, and economic constraints within which individuals are usually confined; identification with "the rest" involves reading one's way through many pages of abuse directed at people like oneself. Unsurprisingly, people of all political persuasions and social positions have more readily discovered themselves to belong to the former category. For who, in the privacy of a reading, can fail to find within themselves some of those qualities of honesty and courage and loftiness of soul that Nietzsche describes?

As Wyndham Lewis observed, there is an element of fairground trickery in this strategy: "Nietzsche, got up to represent a Polish nobleman, with a *berserker* wildness in his eye, advertised the secrets of the world, and sold little vials containing blue ink, which he represented as drops of authentic blue blood, to the delighted populace. They went away, swallowed his prescriptions, and felt very noble almost at once."[13] Put like this, it sounds as though Nietzsche's readers are simply credulous. But there is more to it. Take Stanley Rosen's account of the same phenomenon in Nietzsche-reception: "An appeal to the highest, most gifted human individuals to create a radically new society of artist-warriors was expressed with rhetorical power and a unique mixture of frankness and ambiguity in such a way as to allow the mediocre, the foolish, and the mad to regard themselves as the divine prototypes of the highest men of the future."[14] How many of those who read this statement regard themselves as these "divine prototypes"? Very few I suspect. For in uncovering Nietzsche's rhetorical strategy Rosen reuses it. The juxtaposition of "the highest, most gifted human individuals" to whom Nietzsche addressed himself, and "the mediocre, the foolish, and the mad" who claimed what was not rightfully theirs, encourages readers to distance themselves from the former category and identify with the "gifted human individuals" who, it is implied, passed up the opportunity that Nietzsche offered. Like Lewis, Rosen invites his readers to consider the possibility that Nietzsche is only for the little people, and that being a mere Superman may well be beneath them.

Nietzsche's strategy is one from which it is difficult for readers wholly to disentangle themselves. And in *Nietzsche's Dangerous Game*, Daniel Conway argues that it is just this strategy that is central to Nietzsche's post-Zarathustra philosophy. Isolated, and seemingly ignored, the late Nietzsche desperately needs readers, for otherwise his grandiose claims about the epochal significance of his own philosophy cannot possibly be justified. But insofar as his readers passively accept his critique of earlier philosophy, they will hardly be the "monsters of courage and curiosity" needed to transmit his philosophy to the future. However, if Nietzsche's readers actually embody those adventurous qualities he idealizes, they will quickly detect "his own complicity in the decadence of modernity."[15] Paradoxically, therefore, Nietzscheanism is best preserved through readings which expose Nietzsche's decadence and so make him the first martyr to his own strategy. Indeed, Conway's own practice of "reading Nietzsche against Nietzsche" is, as he acknowledges, one example, and so, according to his own argument, ironically serves to perpetuate a Nietzscheanism without Nietzsche: "the apostasy of his children is never complete. They may turn on him, denounce him, even profane his teachings, but they do so only by implementing the insights and strategies he has bequeathed to them."[16] As a result, one aspect of Nietzsche's programme, his suspicion, is forever enacted against another, his critique of decadence, for the suspicion that unmasks the decadence even of the "master of suspicion" is itself a symptom of decadence waiting to be unmasked by future generations themselves schooled in suspicion by their own decadence.

Although Conway illustrates ways in which both Nietzsche and his "signature doctrines" are potentially the victims of his own strategy, he does little to show how the reader can avoid participating in it. In fact, Conway appears to be deploying a more sophisticated version of the Nietzschean response used by Lewis and Rosen. Rather than simply inviting the reader to think of themselves as being superior to the foolish mediocrities who would be Supermen, Conway encourages the reader to join him in the higher task of unmasking the Supermen, and Nietzsche himself. But is there no way to reject Nietzsche without at the same time demonstrating one's masterly superiority to the herd of slavish Nietzscheans from whom one is distinguishing oneself? Can the reader resist, or at least fail to follow, Nietzsche's injunction: "one must be superior..."?

Reading for Victory

THE ACT OF READING always engages the emotions of readers, and to a large degree the success of any text (or act of reading) depends upon a reader's sympathetic involvement. A significant part of that involvement comes from the reader's identification with individuals or types within the story. People routinely identify with the heroes of narratives, and with almost any character who is presented in an attractive light. This involves "adopting the goals of a protagonist" to the extent that the success or failure of those goals occasions an emotional response in the reader similar to that which might be expected of the protagonist, irrespective of whether the protagonist is actually described as experiencing those emotions.[17] Hence, a story with a happy ending is one in which the reader feels happy because of the hero's success, and a sad story is one in which the protagonist is unsuccessful.

Within this process, readers sometimes identify with the goals of characters who may be in many or all external respects (age, race, gender, class, etc.) dissimilar to themselves. But the goals with which they identify—escaping death, finding a mate, achieving personal fulfilment—are almost always ones shared by the reader in that they reflect rational self-interest. The effect of identifying with the goals of protagonists on the basis of self-interest is that the act of reading becomes an attempt to succeed in the same objectives that the reader pursues in everyday life. Indeed, success in the act of reading may actually serve to compensate the reader for their relative inability to realize those same objectives in their own lives. Hence perhaps the apparent paradox generated by Nietzsche's popularity amongst disadvantaged groups he went out of his way to denigrate. They, too, are reading for victory, struggling to wrest success from the text by making themselves the heroes of Nietzsche's narrative.

Reading for victory is the way Nietzsche himself thought people ought to read. As he noted in *Human, All Too Human:*

> Whoever wants really to get to know something new (be it a person, an event, or a book) does well to take up this new thing with all possible love, to avert his eye quickly from, even to forget, everything about it that he finds inimical, objectionable, or false. So, for example, we give the author of a book the greatest possible head start, and, as if in a race, virtually yearn with pounding heart for him to reach his goal.[18]

When he wrote this, Nietzsche considered that reading for victory was only a device and that reason might eventually catch up. But in his later writings, this possibility is dismissed. Knowledge "works as a tool of power" and so "increases with every increase of power."[19] The reader's yearning for victory is now not a means to knowledge but an example of what knowledge is. Getting to know something is no more than the act of interpreting it to one's own advantage: "The will to power *interprets*...In fact, interpretation is itself a means of becoming master of something."[20]

In this context, reading for victory without regard to the objections or consequences of that reading is more than reading the way we usually read: it is also our first intoxicating taste of the will to power. Not only does reading for victory exemplify the will to power, but in reading Nietzsche our exercise of the will to power is actually rewarded with the experience of power. It is possible to see this happen even in a single sentence. Take Nietzsche's boast in *Ecce Homo*, "I am not a man I am dynamite."[21]

Reading these words, who has not felt the sudden thrill of something explosive within themselves; or, at the very least, emboldened by Nietzsche's daring, allowed themselves to feel a little more expansive than usual? This, after all, is the way we usually read. Even though Nietzsche is attributing the explosive power to himself, not to us, we instantly appropriate it for ourselves.

Here perhaps is the root of Nietzsche's extraordinary bond with his readers. Reading Nietzsche successfully means reading for victory, reading so that we identify ourselves with the goals of the author. In so unscrupulously seeking for ourselves the rewards of the text we become exemplars of the uninhibited will to power. No wonder Nietzsche can so confidently identify his readers with the Supermen. It is not just flattery. If Nietzsche's readers have mastered his text, they have demonstrated just those qualities of ruthlessness and ambition that qualify them to be "masters of the earth." But they have done more than earn a status in Nietzsche's fictional world. In arriving at an understanding of Nietzsche's cardinal doctrine they have already proved it to themselves. Nietzsche persuades by appealing to experience—not to our experience of the world, but our experience as readers, in particular our experience as readers of his text.

Reading Like a Loser

THERE IS AN ALTERNATIVE to reading for victory: reading like a loser. Robert Burton described it and its consequences in the *Anatomy of Melancholy:*

> Yea, but this meditation is that marres all, and mistaken
> makes many men farre worse, misconceaving all they reade
> or heare, to their owne overthrow, the more they search and
> reade Scriptures, or divine Treatises, the more they pussle
> themselves, as a bird in a net, the more they are intangled
> and precipitated into this preposterous gulfe. *Many are called,
> but few are chosen, Mat. 20.16 and 22.14.* With such like places of

Scripture misinterpreted strike them with horror, they doubt presently whether they be of this number or no, gods eternall decree of predestination, absolute reprobation, & such fatall tables they forme to their owne ruine, and impinge upon this rocke of despaire.[22]

Reading to one's own overthrow, to convict oneself from the text is an unusual strategy. It differs equally from the rejection of a text as mistaken or immoral and from the assimilation of a text as compatible with one's own being. Reading like a loser means assimilating a text in such a way that it is incompatible with one's self.

The interpretative challenge presented by the doctrine of predestination is in important respects similar to the one Nietzsche offers his readers. The underlying presupposition of both is that many are called, and few are chosen. One might suppose that the majority of those faced with the doctrine would deduce that they are more likely to be amongst the many than the few. But, just as almost all of Nietzsche's readers identify themselves as being amongst the few who are honest, strong, and courageous, so generations of Christians have discovered themselves to be amongst the few who are "called." The alternative, although seemingly logical, was so rare as to be considered pathological. People were not expected to survive in this state. As Burton noted: "Never was any living creature in such torment…in such miserable estate, in such distresse of minde, no hope, no faith, past cure, reprobate, continually tempted to make away with themselves."[23]

Reading like losers, we respond very differently to the claims Nietzsche makes on behalf of himself and his readers. Rather than reading for victory with Nietzsche, or even reading for victory against Nietzsche by identifying with the slave morality, we read for victory against ourselves, making ourselves the victims of the text. Doing so does not involve treating the text with scepticism or suspicion. In order to read like a loser you have to accept the argument, but turn its consequences against yourself.

So, rather than thinking of ourselves as dynamite, or questioning Nietzsche's extravagant claim, we will immediately think (as we might if someone said this to us in real life) that there may be an explosion; that we might get hurt; that we are too close to someone who could harm us. Reading like losers will make us feel powerless and vulnerable.

The net result, of course, is that reading Nietzsche will become far less pleasurable. When we read that "Those who are from the outset victims, downtrodden, broken—they are the ones, the weakest are the ones who most undermine life"[24] we will think primarily of ourselves. Rather than being an exhilarating vision of the limitless possibilities of human emancipation, Nietzsche's texts will continually remind us of our own weakness and mediocrity, and our irremediable exclusion from the life of joy and careless laughter that is possible only for those who are healthier and more powerful. In consequence, we will never experience the mysterious alchemy of Nietzsche's texts in which the reader reaps the benefits of Nietzsche's doctrine in the act of apprehending it.

How then will we feel about Nietzsche? We might answer the way Nietzsche suggests no one has ever answered: "'I don't like him.'—Why?—'I am not equal to him.'"[25] In any case, we will not be able to look him in the face as he asks us to do.[26] His gaze is too piercing, his presence too powerful. We must lower our eyes and turn away.

The Philistine

READING NIETZSCHE LIKE losers is likely to prove more difficult than we might suppose. It involves more than distancing ourselves from his more extravagant claims; it means that we will find it impossible to identify with any of his positive values. This may prove painful, for some of Nietzsche's values are widely endorsed within contemporary culture, and accepting our inability to share them may count as an intellectual and social failing. This is perhaps most obviously true when it comes to art, the one thing to which Nietzsche consistently ascribed a positive value.

It was in *The Birth of Tragedy* that Nietzsche first articulated the view that life was meaningless and unbearable, and that "it is only as an *aesthetic phenomenon* that existence and the world are eternally *justified*."[27] Although he subsequently distanced himself from this early work, Nietzsche never gave up the idea that art was the one redemptive value in the world, or that "we have our highest dignity in our significance as works of art."[28] In his later writings, the role of art comes to be identified with the will to power. As Nietzsche wrote in a draft for the new preface to *The Birth of Tragedy*:

> Art and nothing but art! It is the great means of making life possible, the great seduction to life, the great stimulant of life.
>
> Art as the only superior counterforce to all will to denial of life, as that which is anti-Christian, anti-Buddhist, antinihilist par excellence.[29]

Whereas other putative sources of value, such as religion and morality and philosophical truth, placed themselves in opposition to life, art was not something that stood over and against life, it was the affirmation of life, and so also life's affirmation of itself.

Nietzsche's later vision of art as the value that supersedes all others has two related elements: the role of the aesthetic as a source of value, and the artist as a creator and embodiment of that value. But if we are reading like losers, we are not going to be able to identify with either of these things. We will think of ourselves as philistines who are unable to appreciate what is supposedly the aesthetic dimension of experience; as people who have no taste or discrimination, no capacity to appreciate what are meant to be the finer things of life. This does not just involve distancing ourselves from the rarified discourse of traditional aesthetics; it means not being able to see the point of avant-gardist repudiations of tradition either.

According to Nietzsche, "the effect of works of art is to *excite the state that creates art*." Being an aesthete is therefore indistinguishable from being an artist, for "All art…speaks only to art-ists."[30] Reading like losers places us outside this equation: unable to appreciate, we are also unable to create. We cannot think of ourselves as original or creative people, or as makers of things that add to the beauty or aesthetic variety of the world. When we read Nietzsche's descriptions of the "inartistic state" that subsists "among those who become impoverished, withdraw, grow pale, under whose eyes life suffers,"[31] we should not hurry to exclude ourselves. In Nietzsche's opinion, *'the aesthetic state…appears only in natures capable of that bestowing and overflowing fullness of bodily vigor…[But] The sober, the weary, the exhausted, the dried-up (e.g., scholars) can receive absolutely nothing from art, because they do not possess the primary artistic force."*[32] "Yes," the loser responds, "that sounds like me."

It may not appear to be a very attractive option, for Nietzsche deliberately makes it as unappealing as possible, but acknowledg-ing a lack of "the primary artistic force" must be the starting point for any anti-Nietzscheanism. Anyone who does not do so retains an important stake in Nietzsche's vision of the future. Receptivity to the aesthetic is the ticket to privilege in Nietzsche's world; the only people liable to suffer from his revaluation of values are those who lack it. Nietzsche may claim that only a select minority are likely to qualify, but in a culture where self-identified philistines are conspicuous by their absence, it is not surprising to discover that Nietzsche's readers have consistently found themselves to be included rather than excluded from his vision of the future.

The Subhuman

TO FIND THE ANTI-NIETZSCHE it is necessary not only to locate oneself out-side contemporary culture, but outside the human species alto-gether. Nietzsche's model for the future of intra-specific relations is based on that of inter-specific relations in the natural world. The underlying analogy is that Superman is to man, as man is to animal. Zarathustra pictures man as "a rope stretched between animal and Superman—a rope over an abyss."[33] The philosopher of the future must walk the tightrope. Unlike those who would rather return to the animal state, the Supermen will establish the same distance between themselves and other humans, as humans have established between themselves and animals:

> All creatures hitherto have created something beyond themselves, and do you want to be the ebb of this great tide and return to the animals rather than overcome man?

> What is the ape to men? A laughing stock or a painful embarrassment. And just so shall man be to the Superman: a laughing stock or a painful embarrassment.[34]

Indeed, Nietzsche repeatedly refers to Supermen as being a different species: "I write for a species of man that does not yet exist: for the 'masters of the earth.'"[35] He was not speaking metaphorically, either. He hoped that the new species might be created through selective breeding, and noted the practical possibility of "international racial unions whose task will be to rear the master race, the future 'masters of the earth.'"[36]

According to Nietzsche, it follows from this that, relative to the Supermen, ordinary mortals will have no rights whatsoever. The Supermen have duties only to their equals, "towards the others one acts as one thinks best."[37] The argument here is also based on interspecific analogies. Nietzsche conceives the difference between man and Superman not only in terms of that between animal and man, but on the model of herd animal and predatory animal. He first introduced the idea in *The Genealogy of Morals*, in a discussion of lambs and birds of prey. Noting that it is hardly strange that lambs bear ill will towards large birds of prey, he argues this is "in itself no reason to blame large birds of prey for making off with little lambs." According to Nietzsche, to do so would be

> To demand of strength that it should *not* express itself as
> strength, that it should not be a will to overcome, overthrow,
> dominate, a thirst for enemies and resistance and triumph,
> makes as little sense as to demand of weakness that it should
> express itself as strength.

The argument hinges on the idea of carnivorousness as an expression of the amorality that is a natural and inescapable feature of interspecific relations. Nietzsche imagines his birds of prey saying "*We* bear them no ill will at all, these good lambs—indeed, we love them; there is nothing tastier than a tender lamb."[38] However it may appear to the lambs, for the carnivore eating them it is not a question of ethics, just a matter of taste. Nietzsche therefore argues that were a comparable divide to exist between two human species, the Supermen and the herd animals who sustain them, relations between the species would also be entirely governed by the tastes of the superior species. Nietzsche does not say whether the Supermen will feast upon their human subordinates, but it is inconceivable that he should have any objection to the practice, save perhaps gastronomic.

Why do not Nietzsche's readers experience the visceral fear of the Superman that Nietzsche attributes to the lambs? The answer is surely that the reader immediately identifies with the human rather than the animal, and with the carnivore rather than the herbivore. Nietzsche's argument relies on the assumption that the patterns of interspecific relations are unquestioned and that it will be easier for the reader to imagine eating other species than it is to imagine being eaten by them. The raptors' response to the lamb is therefore also that of carnivorous readers, who also love lamb as much as they love lambs. Reading like losers, however, we may see things rather differently. We will not just identify with man rather than Superman, but also with the animal rather than man, and with the herd animal rather than the predator. The pattern of interspecific behaviour that Nietzsche describes will immediately strike us as terrifying—an all-out war against the defenceless explicable only in terms of the hatred of the predator for the prey.

Once again, the difficulty of reading like losers is extreme. First, rather than dismissing Nietzsche's suggestion that intrahuman diversity could ever produce distinct species of men and Supermen, we have to accept the idea that interspecific analogues are relevant. Second, we have to relocate ourselves within those analogues in the position of the subhuman rather than the human, as ape to man, herbivore to carnivore. This means divesting ourselves of all our assumptions about species superiority and imagining our experience of the human species to be that of a subhuman species. Consistently thinking about the human from the perspective of the subhuman is difficult, but in reading like a loser we have to give up the idea of becoming more than man and think only of becoming something less.

Nietzsche himself identified becoming subhuman with the egalitarian projects of democracy and socialism:

> The *over-all degeneration of man* down to what today appears to
> the socialist dolts and flatheads as their "man of the future"—
> as their ideal—this degeneration and diminution of man into
> the perfect herd animal (or, as they say, to the man of the "free
> society"), this animalization of man into the dwarf animal of
> equal rights and claims, is possible, there is no doubt of it.

The prospect strikes Nietzsche with horror: "Anyone who has once thought through this possibility to the end knows one kind of nausea that other men don't know."[39] Even those who consider Nietzsche to have offered an absurd caricature of the socialist project would probably agree that the subhumanization of man was a repulsive goal. But if we are reading like losers we may think differently. Just as the superhumanization of man will fill us with terror, the dehumanization of man into a herd animal will strike us as offering a welcome respite from a cruel predator, and opening up new possibilities for subhuman sociality. And although the subhuman, like the philistine, may not seem like the most promising basis for a thoroughgoing anti-Nietzscheanism, it is more than just a hypothetical counter-Nietzschean position generated by a perverse strategy of reading: the subhuman and the philistine are not two forms of the Anti-Nietzsche but one.

Negative Ecology of Value

NIETZSCHE'S PROJECT IS the revaluation of all values. There are two stages: the first nihilistic, the second ecological. Nietzsche acknowledged himself to be "a thorough-going nihilist," and although he says he accepted this only in the late 1880s, the idea obviously appealed, for he then proclaimed himself to be "the first perfect nihilist of Europe who, however, has even now lived through the whole of nihilism, to the end, leaving it behind, outside himself."[40] What Nietzsche means is that he has accepted, more completely than anyone before him, the "absolute untenability of existence when it comes to the highest values one recognizes."[41] All the values of religion and morality which were supposed to make life worth living are unsustainable; scepticism has undermined the lot. The truthfulness enjoined by religion and morality has shown the values of religion and morality (including the value of truth itself) to be fictitious. In this way, the highest values of the past have devalued themselves. Nihilism is not something that has worked against religion and morality, it has worked through them. The advent of nihilism, the realization that everything that was thought to be of value is valueless, therefore represents both the triumph of Christian values and their annihilation. As Heidegger observed, "for Nietzsche, nihilism is not in any way simply a phenomenon of decay; rather nihilism is, as the fundamental event of Western history, simultaneously and above all the intrinsic law of that history."[42]

Although Nietzsche does not repudiate nihilism, he anticipates that in the future it will take another form. He argues that "the universe seems to have lost value, seems 'meaningless'—but that is only a *transitional stage*."[43] What lies beyond it is "a movement that in some future will take the place of this perfect nihilism—but presupposes it, logically and psychologically."[44] The movement is the one that Nietzsche describes as the revaluation of all values. The presupposition of this is that "we require, sometime, *new values*," but not values of the old kind that measure the value of the world in terms of things outside it, for they "refer to a purely fictitious world."[45] Nietzsche's revaluation of values demands more than this, "an overturning of the nature and manner of valuing."[46]

Nietzsche does not use the word, but the form of this revaluation of valuing is perhaps most accurately described as ecological, not because Nietzsche exhibited any particular concern for the natural environment, but on account of the unprecedented conjunction of two ideas: the recognition of the interdependence of values, and the evaluation of value in biological terms. As a pioneer in the study of the history of values, Nietzsche sought "knowledge of their growth, development, displacement."[47] Values did not coexist in an unchanging timeless harmony. Within history some values had displaced others because not all values can simultaneously be equally valuable. Some values negate and devalue others: Christianity had involved "a revaluation of all the values of antiquity." for the ancient values, "pride...the deification of passion, of revenge, of cunning, of anger, of voluptuousness, of adventure, of knowledge," could not prosper in the new moral climate.[48] And the same could happen again: "Moral values have hitherto been the highest values: would anybody call this in question?—If we remove these values from this position, we alter all values: the principle of their order of rank hitherto is thus overthrown."[49] In consequence, the revaluation of values involves not the invention of new values, but reinventing the relationships between the old ones: "The future task of the philosopher: this task being understood as the solution of the *problem of value*, [is] the determination of the *hierarchy of values*."[50]

If it was as a genealogist of values that Nietzsche discovered their precarious ecology, it was as a nihilist that he sought to exploit it. Nietzsche recognized that, just as asserting one value negated another, so the denial of value placed a positive valuation upon the negation itself. The one irreducible value was therefore the value of valuation. But since, for a nihilist, values are valueless in themselves, the value of valuation is not merely the last value but the only one. As Nietzsche states, nihilism "places the value of things precisely in the lack of any reality corresponding to these values and in their being merely a symptom of strength on the part of the value-positers."[51] The effect of this argument is heavily reductive, for if the only value is valuation, then all that is of value is the capacity to establish values, a capacity that Nietzsche equates with life itself: "When we speak of values we do so under the inspiration and from the perspective of life: life itself evaluates through us when we establish values."[52] However, life itself is contested, and so "There is nothing to life that has value except the degree of power—assuming that life itself is the will to power."[53]

As a historian, Nietzsche noted that "Values and their changes are related to increases in the power of those positing the values,"[54] but, according to his own reductive argument, changes in value are not merely related to changes in power, they are themselves those changes in power, for the only value is "the highest quantum of power that a man is able to incorporate."[55] So, because value resides in valuation, and valuation exists only where there is the power to establish values, the ecology of value within the realm of ideas becomes a literal biological ecology of living organisms. As Nietzsche puts it:

> The standpoint of "value" is the standpoint of conditions of preservation and enhancement for complex forms of relative life-duration within the flux of becoming.[56]

In short, value is ultimately ecological, in that what is of value is the conditions that allow valuation. And since, according to

Nietzsche, "it is the intrinsic right of *masters* to create values,"[57] it follows that "'Value' is essentially the standpoint for the increase or decrease of these dominating centres."[58] The future task of the philosopher is therefore that of establishing not so much a hierarchy of value, or even a hierarchy of value-positers, as that of creating an ecology in which valuation is possible. Not being familiar with the twentieth-century concept of the ecologist, Nietzsche imagines a new type of physician whose concern is with the health of society as a whole:

> I am still waiting for a philosophical *physician* in the exceptional sense of that word—one who has to pursue the problem of the total health of a people, time, race or of humanity—to muster the courage to push my suspicion to its limits and to risk the proposition: what was at stake in all philosophizing hitherto was not at all "truth" but something else—let us say, health, future, growth, power, life.[59]

What this global ecologist of value would do is create conditions that foster the production of value-positors. And since the "higher type is possible only through the subjugation of the lower,"[60] this means breeding a master species capable of enslaving the rest of the world:

> a new, tremendous artistocracy, based on the severest self-legislation, in which the will of philosophical men of power and artist-tyrants will be made to endure for millennia—a higher kind of man who . . . employ democratic Europe as their most pliant and supple instrument for getting hold of the destinies of the earth, so as to work as artists upon "man" himself.[61]

In this ecology, the philistine and the subhuman are the same thing. Nietzsche equates receptivity to the aesthetic with being an artist, being an artist with the capacity for valuation, and the capacity for valuation with the exercise of power. Just as his artist-tyrants display their artistry through their tyranny and exercise their tyranny in their artistry, so philistinism is the mark of the subhuman, and subhumanization the fate of the philistine. Because they fail to participate in art, the *"affirmation, blessing, deification,* of existence,"[62] philistines lack will to power, and are enslaved. And because subhumans lack the power to create value, they can never appreciate it either. Within the ecology of value a certain number of subhuman-philistines are always necessary in order to act as slaves to the supermen-aesthetes, but since an ecology of value is one that fosters the production of supermen-aesthetes rather than subhuman-philistines it follows that any increase in the latter, beyond the minimum needed to serve the needs of their masters, will have a negative effect on that ecology. Nietzsche's vision of the future naturally includes provision for the extermination of these vermin, for their proliferation will do more than have a negative effect on his ecology of value; since the ecology of value is the last remaining value in the history of nihilism, its negation is the ultimate negation of value itself.

It is worth considering the implications of this a little further. For a thorough-going nihilist the last value must be derived from the negation of value. Since valuation is unavoidable, it would seem to follow that valuation is that last value. And this is why Nietzsche thinks that the ecology of value will be the ultimate conclusion of his nihilism. But this is not so. Although value might ultimately be ecological, it does not follow that its ecology is valuable. Rather than a positive ecology of value, which creates the possibility for conditions of valuation, there might be a negative ecology. The nihilistic impulse might turn against this last redoubt of value, arguing that the last value must be the negation of the conditions of valuation, an ecology which minimizes the possibilities for the positing of value and so reduces the quantum of value still further. On this view, the last value would not be an ecology of value but a negative ecology of value. The full significance of the philistine and the subhuman now becomes clearer. Reading Nietzsche as a philistine-subhuman is not just a matter of finding a perspective from which Nietzsche's ideas appear alien and threatening, it actually constitutes a counter-move to Nietzsche's strategy. Reading for victory exemplifies the will to power and promotes an ecology of value by increasing the numbers of those who are value-positors; reading like a loser has a direct negative impact on that ecology since it decreases the proportion of value-positors. Taking up the role of the philis-tine-subhuman therefore continues the nihilistic dynamic that Nietzsche thought he had ended, not by perpetuating the *ressenti-ment* of slave-morality—reading like a loser is not an affirmation of the values through which losers become winners—but by hav-ing a direct, negative impact on the ecology of value.

Total Society

IT MIGHT APPEAR that a negative ecology of value could feature on only the most perverse of dystopian agendas. But that would be a hasty judgement. The negative ecology of value, which Nietzsche called "the kingdom of heaven of the poor in spirit," had in his view already begun:

> The French Revolution as the continuation of Christianity.
> Rousseau is the seducer: he again unfetters woman who is
> henceforth represented in an ever more interesting manner—
> as suffering. Then the slaves and Mrs. Beecher-Stowe. Then the
> poor and the workers. Then the vice addicts and the sick . . .
> We are well on the way: the kingdom of heaven of the poor in
> spirit has begun.[63]

The way in which this process served to negate value is spelt out most clearly with regard to slavery: "'Abolition of slavery'—sup-posedly a tribute to 'human dignity,' in fact a destruction of a fundamentally different type (—the undermining of its values and happiness—)."[64] Rather than accepting the rhetoric of lib-eration on its own terms, and seeing it as an extension of the ecology of value which attributes positive qualities to those who are liberated, Nietzsche sees it only as a negation of the values reposed within the masters. Thus, the liberation of women serves only to negate the special value of masculinity; the emancipation of slaves the value of whiteness, the liberation of the workers the value of capital, the liberation of the sick the seemingly unarguable value of health itself.

Those who seek to oppose Nietzsche typically reject his analysis of these changes and maintain that the long process of human emancipation has not only been motivated by the desire to promote values but has also contributed to their ecology. But, as has often been noted, this argument is difficult to sustain at a historical or sociological level. Whatever the intentions of those who have promoted these social reforms, their effect has not been to strengthen value, but rather to dilute it by widening its scope. Durkheim, writing shortly after Nietzsche, was perhaps the first to note the pattern. Laws against murder are now more inclusive than in former times, but

> If all the individuals who…make up society are today protected to an equal extent, this greater mildness in morality is due, not to the emergence of a penal rule that is really new, but to the extension of the scope of an ancient rule. From the beginning there was a prohibition on attempts to take the life of any member of the group, but children and slaves were excluded from this category. Now that we no longer make such distinctions actions have become punishable that once were not criminal. But this is merely because there are more persons in society, and not because collective sentiments have increased in number. These have not grown, but the object to which they relate has done so.[65]

Indeed, as he argued in *The Division of Labour in Society*, the *conscience collective*, the set of values shared by a social group, is progressively weakened by increases in the size and complexity of the unit. Taken to its limits, the dynamic that Durkheim describes involves the totalization of society to its maximal inclusiveness and complexity, and the corresponding elimination of shared values.

Already, he suggests, morality "is in the throes of an appalling crisis."[66] If the totalization of society and the weakening of *la conscience collective* is not balanced by the development of organic solidarity through the division of labour, the change will result only in *anomie*.

Although they emphasize different aspects of the process, it is clear that Durkheim and Nietzsche are addressing the same issue. Both describe the origins of morality in the customs of communities bound together by what Durkheim called "mechanical solidarity." But what is, for Durkheim, the expansion of the group and the weakening of *la conscience collective*, is, for Nietzsche, the slave revolt in morals and the beginnings of European nihilism:

> Refraining mutually from injury, violence, and exploitation and placing one's will on a par with someone else—this may become . . . good manners among individuals if the appropriate conditions are present (namely, if these men are actually similar in strength and value standards and belong together in *one* body). But as soon as this principle is extended, and possibly even accepted as the *fundamental principle of society,* it immediately proves to be what it really is—a will to the *denial* of life, a principle of disintegration and decay.[67]

Durkheim is nervously optimistic about the totalization of society. Observing that "there is tending to form, above European peoples, in a spontaneous fashion, a European society," he argued that even if "the formation of one single human society is forever ruled out—and this has, however, not yet been demonstrated—at least the formation of larger societies will draw us continually closer to that goal."[68] In contrast, Nietzsche's response is to demand a return to mechanical solidarity, not of course for everyone, but for the few strong men who can create value. Only if society is detotalized and redivided into the community of the strong and the undifferentiated mass of the weak can the conditions for value creation be sustained:

> As a good man, one belongs to the "good," a community that has a communal feeling, because all the individuals are entwined together by their feeling for requital. As a bad man, one belongs to the "bad," to a mass of abject, powerless men who have no communal feeling.[69]

In this context, our reading of Nietzsche assumes additional importance. Identifying positively with any narrative (written or otherwise) means making its goals one's own. And although we may not be trying to make common cause with other readers, reading for victory has a strong centripetal dynamic: the greater our success, the more closely our goals converge with those of others who are doing the same thing. Reading Nietzsche for victory is the route to his new mechanical solidarity. In contrast, reading like losers is centrifugal. Since we are not in any sense opposed to the text, we have no common cause even with those who are reading for victory against it, we just become part of that "mass of abject, powerless men who have no communal feeling." Reading like a loser, in its consistent exclusion of the reader from shared value, is a willingness to exchange an exclusive communality for an inclusive and indiscriminate sociality.

Becoming part of a mass with no communal feeling may negate the ecology of value, but such a mass is not necessarily a negative ecology. Like Nietzsche, Durkheim thought of society in biological terms. His model of organic solidarity is an oak tree which can sustain "up to two hundred species of insects that have no contacts with one another save those of good neighbourliness."[70] Just as an environment can sustain a higher population the greater the diversity of the species within it, so society can accommodate more people if they have less in common and more diversified social roles. But whereas Durkheim's ecology is acknowledged to be part of a negative ecology of value, Nietzsche's ecology is a positive ecology of value designed to sustain species whose will to power is value positing:

society must *not* exist for society's sake but only as the founda-
tion and scaffolding on which a choice type of being is able
to raise itself to its higher task and to a higher state of *being*—
comparable to those sun-seeking vines of Java...that so long
and so often enclasp an oak tree with their tendrils until
eventually, high above it but supported by it, they can unfold
their crowns in the open light and display their happiness.[71]

It is Nietzsche's commitment to an ecology of value that makes him
an anti-social thinker. The boundaries of society must be constrict-
ed in order to sustain the flower of value. For the anti-Nietzschean,
however, the argument will go the other way. The boundaries of society must be extended in order to decrease the possibility of value,
for the negative ecology of value is total society.

A Possibility

NIETZSCHE'S IMAGE OF the vine climbing the oak neatly encapsu-
lated his idea that the Supermen must exercise their will to power as parasites upon society. Translating the idea into historical
terms supplied Nietzsche with an extraordinary vision: "I see in
my mind's eye a *possibility* of a quite unearthly fascination and
splendour...a spectacle at once so meaningful and so strange-
ly paradoxical it would have given all the gods of Olympus an
opportunity for an immortal roar of laughter—*Cesare Borgia as
Pope.*"[72] Like the vine that strangles the tree as it reaches toward
the sunlight, Cesare Borgia would have abolished Christianity by
becoming its head.

The totalization of society does not require such fantasies, but
it may involve changes for which many are unprepared. For example, one recent appeal for the ongoing totalization of society is
"The Declaration on Great Apes," which proclaims that

The notion of "us" as opposed to "the other," which like a more
and more abstract silhouette, assumed in the course of centuries the contours of the boundaries of the tribe, of the nation,

of the race, of the human species, and which for a time the species barrier had congealed and stiffened, has again become something alive, ready for further change.

The Declaration looks forward to "the moment when the dispersed members of the chimpanzee, gorilla and orang-utan species can be liberated and lead their different lives as equals in their own special territories in our countries."[73] However, neither the signatories of the Declaration, nor subsequent advocates of simian sovereignty have specified where these simian homelands should be located. It has been suggested that some heavily indebted equatorial nation might be induced to cede part of its territory in return for relief from its creditors.[74] But within a negative ecology of value there may be other, more appropriate solutions.

Even if not undertaken with this intention, extending the boundaries of society to include members of other species is liable to devalue specifically human values, notably those of culture. Not only does it run counter to the Nietzschean argument that (super)humans, as the sole value-creating species, should live in a world that maximizes their capacity to flourish at the expense of other non–value generating species, but by including within society so many unregenerate philistines, it undermines the capacity for human culture to function as a shared value within the expanded society. In such a philistine ecology, some redundant piece of the West's cultural heritage might prove to be a suitable location for an autonomous simian group. Perhaps the Louvre, and its collections, could be put at the disposal of apes freed from zoos and research laboratories: the long galleries could be used for sleeping and recreation, the Jardin des Tuileries for foraging. Who but a Nietzschean could object?

Endnotes

[1] Ishay Landa, "Nietzsche, the Chinese Worker's Friend," *New Left Review* 1, no. 236 (July–August 1999): pp. 3–23.

[2] Alain Boyer, "Hierarchy and Truth," in Luc Ferry and Alain Renaut, eds., *Why We Are Not Nietzscheans* (Chicago, 1997), p. 2.

[3] Geoff Waite, *Nietzsche's Corps/e: Aesthetics, Politics, Prophecy, or, The Spectacular Technoculture of Everyday Life* (Durham, NC, 1996), p. xi.

[4] Waite, *Nietzsche's Corps/e*, p. 67 and p. 232.

[5] Friedrich Nietzsche quoted in ibid., pp. 315–16.

[6] Fredrick Appel, *Nietzsche Contra Democracy* (Ithaca, 1999), p. 2.

[7] Friedrich Nietzsche, *The Will to Power* (hereafter WP), trans. Walter Kaufmann and R. J. Hollingdale (New York, 1967), 872 (unless otherwise indicated, references to Nietzsche's works are to section numbers, not page numbers).

[8] Appel, *Contra Democracy*, p. 167.

[9] Waite, *Nietzsche's Corps/e*, p. 70.

[10] WP, 958.

[11] Waite, *Nietzsche's Corps/e*, p. 24.

[12] Friedrich Nietzsche, *The Anti-Christ*, trans. R. J. Hollingdale (Harmondsworth, 1968), Foreword.

[13] Wyndham Lewis, *The Art of Being Ruled* (Santa Rosa, CA, 1989), p. 113.

[14] Stanley Rosen, *The Ancients and the Moderns* (New Haven, 1989), p. 190.

[15] Daniel Conway, *Nietzsche's Dangerous Game: Philosophy in the Twilight of the Idols* (Cambridge, 1997), p. 152.

[16] Ibid., p. 256.

[17] See Keith Oatley, "A Taxonomy of the Emotions in Literary Response and a Theory of Identification in Fictional Narrative,"*Poetics* 23 (1994): pp. 53–74; D. W. Albritton and R. J. Gerrig found that readers have positive preferences for the outcomes of narratives, and that having negative preferences (e.g., hoping that the protagonist misses a flight) is so unusual that when readers are manipulated into preferring a negative outcome (e.g., by being told that the plane will crash) they are less able to remember the actual outcome; see their "Participatory Responses in Text Understanding," *Journal of Memory and Language* 30 (1991): pp. 603–26.

[18] Friedrich Nietzsche, *Human, All Too Human*, trans. Marion Faber (Harmondsworth, 1984), 621.

[19] WP, 480.

[20] WP, 643.

21 Friedrich Nietzsche, *Ecce Homo,* trans. R. J. Hollingdale (Harmondsworth, 1979), p. 126.

22 Robert Burton, *The Anatomy of Melancholy* (Oxford, 1989), 3:p. 434.

23 Ibid., p. 422.

24 Friedrich Nietzsche, *On the Genealogy of Morals,* trans. Douglas Smith (Oxford, 1996), 3.14.

25 Friedrich Nietzsche, *Beyond Good and Evil* (hereafter BGE), trans. Walter Kaufmann (New York, 1966), 185.

26 Nietzsche, *Anti-Christ,* 1.

27 Friedrich Nietzsche, *The Birth of Tragedy,* trans. Walter Kaufmann (New York, 1967), 5; see also Nietzsche, *The Gay Science,* trans. Walter Kaufmann (New York, 1974), 107.

28 Nietzsche, *Birth of Tragedy,* 5.

29 WP, 853.

30 WP, 809 and 821.

31 WP, 812.

32 WP, 801.

33 Friedrich Nietzsche, *Thus Spoke Zarathustra,* trans. R. J. Hollingdale (Harmondsworth, 1969), p. 43.

34 Ibid., p. 41.

35 WP, 958.

36 WP, 960.

37 WP, 943.

38 Nietzsche, *Genealogy,* 1.13.

39 Nietzsche, *Beyond Good and Evil,* 203.

40 WP, Prologue, 2.

41 WP, 3.

42 Martin Heidegger, *The Question Concerning Technology* (New York, 1977), p. 67.

43 WP, 7.

44 WP, Prologue, 2.

45 WP, 12B.

46 Heidegger, *Concerning Technology,* p. 70.

47 Nietzsche, *Genealogy,* Preface, 6.

48 WP, 221.

[49] WP, 1006.

[50] Nietzsche, *Genealogy,* 1.17.

[51] WP, 13.

[52] Friedrich Nietzsche, *The Twilight of the Idols,* trans., R. J. Hollingdale (Harmondsworth, 1968), 5:45.

[53] WP, 55.

[54] WP, 14.

[55] WP, 714.

[56] WP, 715.

[57] BGE, 261.

[58] WP, 715.

[59] Nietzsche, *Gay Science,* 35.

[60] WP, 660.

[61] WP, 960.

[62] WP, 821.

[63] WP, 94.

[64] WP, 315.

[65] Emile Durkheim, *The Division of Labour in Society,* trans. W. D. Halls (London, 1984), p. 117.

[66] Ibid., p. 339.

[67] BGE, 259.

[68] Durkheim, *Division of Labour,* p. 337.

[69] Nietzsche, *All Too Human,* 45; see also, Nietzsche, *Genealogy,* 1.11.

[70] Durkheim, *Division of Labour,* p. 209.

[71] Nietzsche, *Good and Evil,* 258.

[72] Nietzsche, *Anti-Christ,* 61.

[73] Paola Cavalieri and Peter Singer, eds., *The Great Ape Project* (London, 1993), p. 5 and p. 6.

[74] See Robert E. Goodin, Carole Pateman, and Roy Pateman, "Simian Sovereignty," *Political Theory* 25 (1997): pp. 821–49.

Malcolm Bull

Nietzsche's Negative Ecologies

> *The desert is growing. How far can it spread?*
> —Ernst Jünger

NIETZSCHE'S TREATMENT OF nihilism is often surprising, not least for its transformation of a relatively recent neologism into a world-historical category. The word was originally used as a derogatory term for post-Kantian idealism, which treated the thing-in-itself as nothing, and later to refer to various strands of Left Hegelianism. Only with the portrayal of Bazarov in Turgenev's *Fathers and Sons*, published in 1862, did the concept gain wider currency.[1] The assassination of Tsar Alexander II in 1881 added a political urgency, and it was in the years following this event, to which he alludes as "nihilism à la Petersburg (meaning the *belief in unbelief* even to the point of martyrdom)," that Nietzsche turned his attention to the topic.[2]

He was not alone. In the 1880s, nihilism was the subject of perhaps a dozen books published in Germany and the topic of excitable commentary throughout Europe and the United States. Nietzsche's interest should therefore be seen in the context of a wave of international anxiety akin, perhaps, to the fascination with Islamic terrorism since 2001. This, too, had racial undertones: the *New York Times* described the Russian nihilists as "Asiatic Nomads seeking to destroy Western Civilization," and there was frequent reference to their "Tartar" origins.[3] Describing Bakunin, Jean Richepin offered the view that "this man was certainly not a European, a Slav, a child of the Aryan deists, but a descendant of the atheist hordes who have nearly destroyed our world several times already, and who, instead of the idea of progress, carry the idea of nothingness buried in their hearts."[4]

Above all, the sudden eruption of this new threat to the established order required explanation, and this was also Nietzsche's question: "Nihilism is standing at the gate: from where does this uncanniest of guests come to us?"[5] But his answer is novel. Unlike his contemporaries, he finds the origins of nihilism not on some remote steppe but within European civilization, and not among the conquering hordes, but in what he calls "the slave morality." For Nietzsche it is "the inexorable progress of the morality of compassion…the most uncanny symptom of the uncanny development of our European culture" that has led toward nihilism.[6] The explanation for its appearance lies in the Christian-moral interpretation of the world.[7]

Why should Christianity result in nihilism? What Nietzsche calls "the first nihilism" is simple pre-ideological despair induced by the hardships and uncertainties of existence. Christian morality was "the great *antidote*" to such nihilism in that "it shielded man from despairing of himself as man" by affirming the existence of another world and a set of values at odds with those of this world.[8] But at the same time it also acted as "a stimulus to nihilism," for by positing a "true world" in opposition to this one, Christianity was itself an "attempt to overcome, i.e., to negate the world."[9]

In so doing, Christian morality also potentially legitimated the critique of its own otherworldly values in the name of truthfulness. Such a critique was inevitable because the values of Christian morality are self-denying, and the only consistent alternatives are either to renounce those values or to renounce the self. Hence the appearance of what Nietzsche termed "the terrifying Either/ Or" that might confront coming generations: "'Either abolish your reverences or—*yourselves*!' The latter would be nihilism; but would not the former also be—nihilism?—This is *our* question mark."[10]

Much of Nietzsche's later writing is an attempt to resolve this dilemma: how to find a route out of nihilism that is not itself nihilistic. Finding such a route is difficult for two reasons: on the one hand, because nihilism is not yet completed, attempts to end it may serve only to effect its continuation; on the other, because it has more than one form, attempts to evade one may fall into the embrace of the other.

Nietzsche claims that there are degrees of nihilism, that it is increasing and that the increase is inevitable. Although we live, at present, in the midst of what he calls "incomplete" nihilism, "complete nihilism is the necessary consequence of the ideals entertained hitherto."[11] Nihilism works through history because it has an inexorable internal logic. It represents "the ultimate logical conclusion of our great values and ideals."[12] The history of the next two centuries can be related in advance for "necessity itself is at work here." Attempts to escape nihilism without revaluing our values so far "produce the opposite, make the problem more acute."[13] This process will inevitably continue until we reach the most extreme nihilism, one that "places the *value* of things precisely in the fact that *no* reality corresponds…to that value, which is instead only a symptom of force on the part of the *value-positers*."[14] Only then, when nihilism is complete, will it become possible to move beyond it.

If it is impossible to go beyond nihilism until it is complete, how does Nietzsche think it is to be completed? Although he does not always differentiate between them, Nietzsche suggests that throughout nihilism's history there are two tracks. On the one hand, there is "[n]ihilism as a sign of the *increased power of the spirit*: as **active nihilism**," on the other, "[n]ihilism as a *decline and retreat of the spirit's power:* **passive nihilism**." Active nihilism "may be a sign of *strength*: the force of the spirit may have grown so much that the goals it has had *so far* ('convictions,' articles of faith) are no longer appropriate." Passive nihilism, on the other hand, may be seen as "a sign of weakness: the force of the spirit may be wearied, *exhausted,* so that the goals and values that have prevailed *so far* are no longer appropriate and no longer believed."[15] In the former case, strength has increased to the extent that "it no longer requires these total interpretations, and introductions of meaning," whereas in the latter there is no longer enough "creative strength to create meaning."[16]

The distinction between active and passive nihilism also has a historical dimension, in that both forms are susceptible to differences of degree. There are thus four ideal types of nihilism: incomplete passive, incomplete active, complete passive, and complete active. Although Nietzsche does not set them out systematically, and his vocabulary contains considerable ambiguity, all four types appear within his writings: incomplete passive nihilism is represented by Christianity; incomplete active nihilism is referred to as "active nihilism"; a more complete passive nihilism is found in Buddhism; while a completed active nihilism, sometimes referred to as "extreme nihilism," is embodied by the Superman, Nietzsche's metaphor for the "higher type" of the future.[17] The four ideal types potentially generate six points of comparison, and we can use this rubric to contextualize Nietzsche's repeated contrasts between them.[18]

Christianity v. Active Nihilism. The primary distinction between passive and active nihilism, as it exists in the present, is between Christianity as an incomplete form of passive nihilism that still retains an adherence to values, in this case the values of the weak; and the incomplete active nihilism that has developed from it, as a result of the rejection of those values.

According to Nietzsche, "Christianity…is in the profoundest sense nihilistic," and were Jesus to appear in Europe today, he might "live, teach, and speak as a nihilist."[19] It is nihilistic insofar as it denies this world and the natural values of the strong. For "those who have come off badly," Christian morality is a form of protection against despair at their own oppression. Instead, it induces despair in the strong, who then end up denying Christian values rather than themselves. This is active nihilism, and the context in which this appears is the opposite of that which gave rise to passive nihilism. Whereas Christianity is a remedy applied at profound levels of misery, active nihilism appears under conditions that are much more favorable.[20]

This explains the appearance of active nihilism in contemporary Europe, where the extreme position represented by Christianity has been replaced not by "a moderated one but by a new extreme one, its *converse*."[21] This is the nihilism that "is standing at the gate," created by "a backlash from 'God is truth' into the fanatical belief 'Everything is false.'"[22]

Christianity v. Buddhism. As Nietzsche makes clear, Christianity is not the only nihilistic religion. All religion is, by definition, nihilistic, but the other faith with which he compares Christianity is Buddhism. Christianity and Buddhism have some important things in common. Both are forms of passive nihilism in that they implicitly or explicitly agree that it is "better not to be than to be,"[23] and both are said to have "owed their origin and above all their sudden spread to a tremendous collapse and disease of the will."[24]

From the *Birth of Tragedy* onwards, Buddhism is associated with the negation of the will, and, following Max Müller's essay on Buddhist nihilism of 1869, Nietzsche identifies this negation with nihilism.[25] However, whereas Christianity had tried and failed to produce an antidote to nihilism through establishing an alternative system of values, Buddhism has moved beyond values altogether: "Buddhism … no longer speaks of 'the struggle against *sin*' but, quite in accordance with actuality, 'the struggle against *suffering'*... it stands, in my language, *beyond* good and evil."[26]

Christianity represents the perspective of an "unproductive, suffering kind, a kind weary of life" who think that "this world, in which we live, is an error—this world of ours ought not to exist" but nevertheless maintain that "the world as it ought to be exists." In contrast, Buddhism represents "the same species of man, grown one stage poorer, [who] no longer possessing the strength to interpret, to create fictions," has become a thorough-going nihilist, that is, "a man who judges of the world as it is that it ought *not* to be, and of the world as it ought to be that it does not exist."[27]

Buddhism therefore represents a move toward the completion of passive nihilism. Whereas Christianity established civilization as a means of taming the strong, "Buddhism is a religion for the end and fatigue of a civilisation."[28] Its reemergence in Europe portends a "nihilistic catastrophe that puts an end to earthly culture."[29]

Active Nihilism v. Buddhism. Buddhism differs from Christianity in its refusal of substitute values in favor of a direct negation of valuation itself. But if, on the one hand, Buddhism is an emancipation from value, it is also a renunciation of the active destruction of value. It therefore differs from active nihilism both in that active nihilism is concerned with the negation of values and in that it "achieves its *maximum* of relative force as a violent force of *destruction*." The opposite of such active nihilism is a "weary nihilism that no longer attacks: its most celebrated form Buddhism: as passivist nihilism."[30]

This is a confusing distinction because in some places Nietzsche uses Buddhism simply as a synonym for nihilism, as, for example, when he complains that the howling "anarchist dogs" and democratic socialists alike threaten Europe with "a new Buddhism."[31] In other places, he actually imagines a European Buddhism that takes the form of active nihilism. Where Nietzsche describes "Nihilism...standing at the gate," he is thinking of the "backlash from 'God is truth' into the fanatical belief 'Everything is false.' Buddhism of the *deed*...."[32] What does this mean? Quite obviously not a passive nihilism, like classical Buddhism, that implies "one must not act,"[33] but rather an active nihilism of a particular kind, *"Buddhismus der That,"* "Buddhism of the deed," an unmistakable reference to the anarchist tactic of "propaganda of the deed," *"Propaganda der That."*

Nevertheless, both these forms of nihilism are routes to annihilation. Buddhism directly through the will to nothingness, active nihilism indirectly through deliberate provocation: These are the nihilists that "destroy in order to be destroyed...and themselves *want* to have *power* by *forcing* the powerful to become their executioners. This is the European form of Buddhism, *doing No* after all existence has lost its 'meaning,'" represented by those St. Petersburg nihilists who Nietzsche said had taken "belief in unbelief even to the point of martyrdom."[34]

Superman v. Buddhism. Nietzsche differentiates between forms of nihilism in terms of the diverging responses to "the world as is," on the one hand, and "the world as it ought to be" on the other. Christianity answers No to the first and Yes to the second. Active nihilism and Buddhism respond negatively to both. But the Superman says Yes to the world as it is and No to the world as it ought to be—a move that effectively overcomes the distinction between the two by implying that the world is already as it ought to be.

This is the significance of eternal return, "existence as it is, without meaning or goal, but inevitably recurring," a doctrine Nietzsche repeatedly refers to as "the most extreme form of nihilism.[35] It presupposes the denial of "the world as it ought to be" made by Buddhists and active nihilists alike but at the same time opens the way for a more positive response to the world as it is:

> [W]hoever has really . . . looked into, down into the most
> world-denying of all possible ways of thinking—beyond good

and evil and no longer, like the Buddha and Schopenhauer, under the spell and delusion of morality—may just thereby, without really meaning to do so, have opened his eyes to the opposite ideal: the ideal of the most high-spirited, alive, and world-affirming human being who has not only come to terms and learned to get along with whatever was and is, but who wants to have *what was and is* repeated into all eternity.[36]

Buddhism had moved beyond value to valuation but, faced with the terrible possibility of eternal recurrence, had chosen annihilation, the denial of valuation itself. In contrast, the Superman embraces valuation in the full awareness that there are no values, and no possibility that the world will ever be other than it is.

Superman v. Active Nihilism. The doctrine of eternal recurrence also serves to distinguish the active nihilist from the Superman. In the context of eternal recurrence, "coming off badly" takes on a new significance. No longer simply a matter of political domination, it also refers to those who are psychologically or, as Nietzsche has it, "physiologically" unable to cope with the idea: "[T]hey will feel belief in eternal recurrence to be a curse, struck by which one no longer shrinks from any action."[37]

Active nihilism may, as Nietzsche claims, be a sign of strength relative to the weakness of passive nihilism, but it is, simultaneously, "a sign that one's strength is *insufficient* to productively posit for oneself a new goal, a 'Why?', a belief." It "represents a pathological *intermediate state*... because the productive forces are not yet strong enough."[38] If they were stronger, they would be able to move beyond values, for "[i]t is a measure of the degree of strength of will to what extent one can do without meaning in things."[39]

The Superman therefore differs from the active nihilist in the same way that the Buddhist differs from the Christian: the Christian and active nihilist are still concerned with values, while the Buddhist and the Superman have moved beyond values to valuation. However, whereas the Buddhist moves beyond the Christian because he no longer possesses the strength for valuation, the Superman moves beyond the values because he has greater strength, which allows him to posit values in the face of eternal valuelessness.

Christianity v. Superman. Because the Superman combines maximum strength and maximum negativity, he is doubly differentiated from Christianity, which is characterized by a system of values generated by weakness. It is the Superman's strength that allows him to do without values, accept that "valuation itself is only this will to power," and nevertheless go on valuing. Indeed where value is "merely a symptom of strength on the part of the value-positers," it could not be otherwise.[40]

This is why Nietzsche answers the question "Who will prove to be the *strongest?*" with the surprising but, to his liberal admirers, reassuring reply, "[t]he most moderate, those who have no *need* for extreme articles of faith." However, this is not "a new philosophy of modesty"[41] but, as its context within the Lenzer Heide fragment (Nietzsche's most sustained meditation on nihilism) makes clear, the acceptance of the most extreme hypothesis of all.

The history of nihilism is, for Nietzsche, the history of extremity. To the first nihilism of routine suffering, Christianity had offered an alternative, "God." This was "far too extreme a hypothesis," but it was replaced by one that was equally extreme, the "[i]n vain" of "present [that is, active] nihilism." Taken to its logical conclusion this "in vain" is expressed in the doctrine of eternal recurrence, "the most extreme form of nihilism."[42]

Faced with meaninglessness eternally, the strongest are those who can accept it, without any correspondingly extreme reaction. Their moderation consists in their ability to live with eternal recurrence without direct or mediated self-destruction, without succumbing either to the Buddhist will to nothingness or to the active nihilists' compulsion to bring about their own execution.

It is in this, and this alone, that the moderation of the strongest is to be found.

The most moderate are therefore to be found not between extremes, but at the furthest extreme, for they alone can live with the most extreme hypothesis (eternal recurrence). Hence Nietzsche can elsewhere describe the same position in terms of its extremity:

> We immoralists—today we are the only power which needs no allies to reach victory: that makes us by far the strongest amongst the strong. . . . A strong seduction fights for us. . . . The magic that fights for us, the eye of Venus that ensnares and blinds even our opponents, is the *magic of the extreme*, the seduction that every extreme exercises: we immoralists, we are *extreme*.[43]

Where does Nietzsche locate himself within this history? In several places at once: both before and after nihilism, sometimes anticipating its arrival, as European culture moves "in what direction? Towards a new Buddhism? Towards a European Buddhism? Towards—*nihilism*?" sometimes awaiting its end, and the "man of the future, who will redeem us…from the will to nothingness, from nihilism"; sometimes looking back over its completed history, describing himself as "the first perfect nihilist of Europe who, however, has even now lived through the whole of nihilism, to the end, leaving it behind, outside himself."[44]

He writes in a sort of now-time where all options are simultaneously available: "a soothsayer-bird spirit who *looks back* when relating what will come." He does not place himself within a linear process, so much as in a complex relation to a multiplicity of points, contrasting his revaluation of all values with its predecessor, active nihilism, its putative rival, the passive nihilism of Buddhism, and, above all, with its double opposite, the passive nihilism of Christianity with which it has neither activity nor the (dis)value of valuation in common.

The progression from incomplete to completed nihilism and beyond is also temporal. The first phase, that of incompleted nihilism, is a phase of values: the negative values of Christian morality and the negation of those values by active nihilists. The former have been dominant for almost two millennia, but, as events in Russia suggest, the latter is already emerging as a counterstrategy. The second phase, in which nihilism is completed, is concerned with valuation rather than values. Although something like the Buddhist negation of the will has already been espoused by Schopenhauer, Nietzsche clearly thinks of this as an as yet unrealized, terminal phase of European civilization. But this too could be a transitional stage:

> Every major growth is accompanied by a tremendous crumbling and passing away: suffering, the symptoms of decline *belong* in the times of tremendous advances; every fruitful and powerful movement of humanity has also created at the same time a nihilistic movement. It could be the sign of a crucial and most essential growth, of the transition to new conditions of existence, that the most extreme form of pessimism, genuine *nihilism*, would come into the world.[45]

Nietzsche plans to move beyond it while presupposing it: "Such an experimental philosophy as I live anticipates experimentally even the possibilities of the most fundamental nihilism; but this does not mean that it must halt at a negation, a No, a will to negation. It wants rather to cross over to the opposite of this—to a Dionysian affirmation of the world as it is."[46] Those who can face eternal recurrence without either the Buddhist longing for annihilation on the one hand, or the active nihilist destructive self-destruction on the other, will finally have left nihilism behind.

What does nihilism mean? That "the highest values devaluate themselves."[47] The history of nihilism's completion is therefore the story of the progressive devaluation of value. But how does that history relate to the history of value itself? Does the renunciation of value make the world any more or less valuable? Although the set of opinions about the amount of value in the world may be quite independent of the actual value of the world, in Nietzsche's account they cannot be separated. Accepting the consequences of nihilism means accepting that the world has no value except that imputed to it, and that value is merely a "symptom of strength on the part of value-positers." The history of value therefore dissolves into the history of valuation, and valuation into life, for valuation is only will to power, and will to power is "life itself." [48]

However, it does not automatically follow that the spread or completion of nihilism diminishes the value of the world. Nietzsche is adamant that *the total value of the world cannot be evaluated.*[49] He offers two justifications for this claim. First, that "there is no 'totality,'" and no evaluation can be made "in regard to something that does not exist."[50] On this view, the world as a whole has no summative value, because the herd, "the *sum of zeroes*" counts for nothing in itself, and "the value of the units determines the significance of the sum."[51] Second, that even if one could speak of a totality, its total value would necessarily be constant or unknowable; given that "becoming has equal value at every moment: the sum of its value remains the same, *in other words it has no value at all.*"[52]

Although there may be no totality because mankind is not a whole, there is, nevertheless, a system in which the ascent of one unit is related to the descent of others, "an inextricable multiplicity of ascending and descending life-processes."[53] There is no total value but there is what Nietzsche terms a "general economy of the whole."[54] How does this work? It is, in the most literal sense, a set of zero-sum relationships. When a lower type ascends, it happens at the expense of the strong.[55] So the abolition of slavery, "supposedly a tribute to human dignity, [is] in fact a destruction of a fundamentally different type."[56] In effect, the value of an ascending type can be measured by the extent of the suffering that makes his ascent possible: "slavery and the division of labour: the higher type possible only through the subjugation of the lower."[57] For this reason, "in the general economy of the whole the terrible aspects of reality are to an incalculable degree more necessary."[58]

For Nietzsche, there are no values as such, and the totality of value is the totality of valuation. There is no way to evaluate the total value of the world itself, but there are ways of measuring fluctuations in the totality of valuation in the world. Valuation is life itself, and within this totality the units that count are those in ascent. Since ascent is relative to that over which there is ascendancy, the value of any unit is derived from the cost to others. Unlike the exploiters, the exploited and the unexploited are zeroes who count for nothing in themselves. If the numbers of those exploited remains the same, then the total value of the whole remains constant. But where there is less than maximal exploitation, then the value in, but not strictly of, the totality is less than it could be.

Nietzsche's account of nihilism is therefore synchronic as well as diachronic. Putting the diachronic and the synchronic together, the transition from incomplete to a complete nihilism represents a movement within the economy of value. It is an economy realized through the ecology of living beings, so the history of nihilism is the history of populations living together across time. Changes in the extent and nature of nihilism come about through the disappearance, destruction, or development of different types of nihilist, and it is through that ecology that the history of nihilism is played out.

Nietzsche makes several explicit references to the way this ecology works. The first offers an explanation of the causes of nihilism:

> 1. *lack of the higher species*, i.e., the one whose inexhaustible fruitfulness and power sustains belief in humanity [for example, Napoleon]....

> 2. *the lower species*, "herd," "mass," "society," forgets how to be modest, and puffs up its needs into *cosmic* and *metaphysical* values. Through this the whole of existence is *vulgarised*: for to

the degree that the *mass* rules, it tyrannises the *exceptions*, who thus lose their belief in themselves and become *nihilists*.[59]

Whereas in this example Nietzsche describes a situation in which the demographic imbalance between the higher and the lower species results in the spread of nihilism amongst the former, in the second, he describes the point at which nihilism is reached, and "all one has left are the values that pass judgement—nothing else." This has differing effects on those with differing degrees of strength:

1. The weak perish of it

2. those who are stronger destroy what does not perish

3. those who are strongest overcome the values that pass judgement[60]

So although nihilism is caused by the preponderance of lower types, it results in their destruction. This is especially true of the most extreme nihilism embodied in the doctrine of eternal recurrence:

> The *most unhealthy* kind of man in Europe (in all classes) is fertile ground for this nihilism; they will feel belief in eternal recurrence to be a *curse*, struck by which one no longer shrinks from any action: not passively dying down, but *extinguishing* everything which lacks aim and meaning in this degree: although it's only a convulsion, a blind rage at the insight that everything has existed for eternities—including this moment of nihilism and lust for destruction.—The *value of such a crisis* is that it *cleanses*, that it crowds related elements together and has them bring about each other's destruction…bringing to light the weaker, more uncertain of them as well and thus initiating *an order of rank among forces*, from the point of view of health: recognising those who command as commanders, those who obey as obeyers.[61]

The weak are the passive nihilists, "passively dying down"; those who are stronger and destroy what does not spontaneously perish are the active nihilists who no longer shrink from any action but "destroy in order to be destroyed."[62] Those who command are those whose acceptance of eternal recurrence allows them to survive the crisis, the Supermen.

The crisis is not exclusively intellectual. Being active means "reaching out for power," being passive means "being hindered in one's forward reaching movement."[63] The two movements are related: reaching out for power involves hindering others, being hindered means being hindered by others. The one necessarily implies the other: "What do *active* and *passive* mean? If not becoming *master* and being *defeated*?"[64] These are, however, trajectories, not identities. Becoming master and being defeated are not just relational but purely relational: the strong are strong only insofar as they gain ascendancy over the weak; the weak are weak just in that they are defeated.

After "the period of catastrophe" and the "advent of a doctrine that sifts men,"[65] there will, Nietzsche hopes, be a third ecology—one where differential breeding maintains a more stable balance between higher and lower types. Here too, Nietzsche thinks in terms of the totality: "To what end shall 'man' as a whole—and no longer as a people, a race—be raised and trained"?[66] His consistent answer is that "perfecting consists in the production of the most powerful individuals, who will use the great mass of people as their tools."[67] So the only uncertainty is "[t]o what extent a sacrifice of freedom, even enslavement, provides the basis for the emergence of a higher type. How could one sacrifice the development of mankind to help a higher species than man come into existence?"[68]

His suggestion is to take advantage of the "dwarfing and adaptation of man to a specialized utility" effected by capitalist modernity and use this as a base on which to create a higher form of mankind:

> This higher form of aristocratism is that of the future.—In
> moral terms, this . . . represents a maximum point in the ex-
> ploitation of man: but it presupposes a kind of men for whose

sake the exploitation has meaning. Otherwise, indeed, it would be just the overall reduction, *value* reduction of the human type—a phenomenon of retrogression in the grandest style.[69]

This, then, is Nietzsche's third ecology. The first, which generated (passive) nihilism, was produced by an excess of lower types; the second, the crisis of nihilism, prompted by the emergence of some stronger types (active nihilists), serves to get rid of that excess through a mix of voluntary and involuntary annihilation; the third embodies the productive equilibrium represented by maximal exploitation.

Each of these is an example of an ecology of value in the sense that it generates certain positions within the history of values that is nihilism, but it is also an ecology of value, insofar as it appears that an ecology is, for Nietzsche, what value ultimately is— not a set of values, or even of valuations, but rather a set of circumstances:

> The viewpoint of "value" is the viewpoint of *conditions of preservation and enhancement* in regard to complex forms of relative life-duration within becoming....
>
> —"Dominating forms"; the sphere of that which dominates continually growing or periodically increasing or decreasing according to the favourability or unfavourability of circumstances
>
> —"Value" is essentially the standpoint for the increase or decrease of these dominating centres[70]

What are these dominating forms, *Herrschaftsgebilde*? Elsewhere, Nietzsche specifically distinguishes the "theory of dominating forms" from mere "sociology," which was, he said, "the sum of zeroes."[71] The theory of dominating forms is the theory of the forms created by the trajectories that count, trajectories of ascent. But the forms to which he refers are not individual trajectories themselves, but rather the shapes collectively created by them.

Such forms are not unities but "multiplicities" made up of infinitely divisible "points of will constantly augmenting or losing their power."[72]

However, such dominating forms do take on definable shapes. Nietzsche sometimes used the word *Herrschaftsgebilde* to refer to the priestly power structures of the Christian church,[73] but his primary point of reference is the new aristocracy of the future. There are, he suggests, "two futures for humanity": one, "the consequence of mediocratisation," the other, "conscious distinction, self-shaping." The latter "preserves the *uppermost and* the *lowest* species (and destroys the middle one)." The theory of "dominating forms" is therefore a theory of aristocracy; the perspective of value is that of the waxing and waning of the uppermost species relative to the lowest, and a positive ecology of value is one that provides the conditions for the preservation and enhancement of a new aristocracy, as opposed to the "value reduction" effected by mediocratization.

Nietzsche predicts just such a positive ecology: "From now on there will be more favourable preconditions for more comprehensive forms of domination, whose like has never yet existed. And even this is not the most important thing; the possibility has been established for the production of international racial unions whose task will be to rear a master race, the future 'masters of the earth.'"[74] As the *Genealogy of Morals* makes clear, these two possibilities are not at odds, for it is usually "some horde or other of blond predatory animals, a race of conquerors and masters" that becomes "a *living* form of domination," spontaneously shaping both themselves and the shapeless mass of the population. Themselves a work of art without an artist,[75] these dominating forms are also "the most involuntary, most unconscious artists," who work "as artists on 'man' himself."[76]

Value, Nietzsche claims, is "the standpoint for the increase or decrease of these dominating centres" realized just insofar as there are "more favourable preconditions for more comprehensive forms of domination." It is to this possibility that he refers when he writes that "the world might be far more valuable than we used to believe." The source of added value is the doctrine of eternal return: "That which set apart the higher men from the lower, the desires that create clefts."[77] Nihilism, the devaluation of existing values that culminates in the doctrine of eternal return, therefore ultimately has the paradoxical effect of bringing about a revaluation in which the value of the world is recognized to be the positive ecology of value brought about by nihilism itself.

This ecology permits Nietzsche to emerge from nihilism. Yet moving beyond completed nihilism is a double maneuver: it is not in value positing that value ultimately resides, but (and this is the bit his defenders do not like) in the particular ecology that allows it. Why? One overcomes nihilism by disregarding value and placing a positive valuation upon valuation. Valuing is will to power, which means power over; hence, there can be no value where there is no power over. This necessarily means that there is more value in an unequal society than in an equal one. Those who value valuation are the new aristocracy, but the value of their valuation of valuation lies not in that valuation itself but in the social arrangement it effects, which is the only one that permits valuation to take place at all.

Although Nietzsche locates this ecology beyond the history of nihilism, further developments within that ecology might reopen the story. Nietzsche's great insight is that nihilism is the product of failure as much as skepticism. On the one hand, it is part of the history of a skepticism propelled by the logic of negation; on the other, it is part of a negative ecology, the unintended consequence of failure. To the question, how far can the desert spread? there are potentially two answers: until there is nothing left to negate and until the conditions are maximally unconducive to value positing.

These are not mutually exclusive possibilities, for one produces the other. It is an important part of Nietzsche's critique of existing values that he reveals that their latent function is to have a negative effect on the ecology of value, and he implicitly (or explicitly) makes this his central argument against them. At the same time, he suggests that they are the consequence of a particular ecology. Nietzsche offers more than one account of this process, a process that provides a model for what could be a fourth ecology, a negative ecology, not of value but of valuation.

A negative ecology is produced by the logic of negation represented since the French revolution by anarchists, peaceful revolutionaries, and socialists who "are at one…in their thoroughgoing and instinctive hostility to every other form of society except that of the *autonomous* herd (even to the point of repudiating the very concepts of master and servant)."[78] However, it is also the consequence of the formation of such a society, in that such revolutionary doctrines embody just the degree of skepticism necessary to justify and protect the herd of human failures. Socialism is "the logical conclusion of the *tyranny* of the least and the dumbest"; in which "is hidden, rather badly, a 'will to negate life.'"[79] The two go together: "[T]o us the democratic movement is not only a form of decay of political organization but a form of the decay, namely the diminution of man, making him mediocre and lowering his value."[80]

For Nietzsche, the present ecology is characterized by its mixed character: on the one hand there is continuing exploitation, but on the other the morality of compassion has led to the enervation of the strong and the proliferation of lower types. From this position he envisages two alternative futures: a great crisis that leads to a new positive ecology of optimal exploitation, or else a further reduction in exploitation and the resulting spread of mediocrity.

In the former case, extermination is necessary because "the great majority of men have no right to existence, but are a misfortune to higher men."[81] A surplus of unexploited lower types is a negative weight on the total ecology, not only because it will reduce the total amount of exploitation, but also because it may diminish the proportion of exploitation within the society in question and thus change its composition and moral character.[82]

Moving toward a positive ecology means reducing that surplus. In the latter case, the proliferation of lower types reduces the proportion of units that count, leaving only what Nietzsche calls "the tremendous surplus of failures: a field of ruins."[83] One future leads toward the extermination of lower types, the other to their proliferation.

Nietzsche considers the latter a real possibility:

> [T]he over-all degeneration of man down to what today appears to the socialist dolts and flatheads as their "man of the future"—as their ideal—this degeneration and diminution of man into the perfect herd animal (or, as they say, the man of the "free society"), this animalization of man into the dwarf animal of equal rights and claims, is possible.[84]

But how? Although Nietzsche does not appear to have considered its consequences at the time, he described such a move in the prologue to *Zarathustra*. Observing the tightrope walker, Zarathustra says, "Man is a rope, fastened between animal and Superman—a rope over an abyss." At one end is the Superman, at the other the Last Man. Having delivered his prophetic vision of the Superman, Zarathustra warns the crowd that although there is still time for the vision to be fulfilled, it will not always be so: "[T]he soil is still rich enough for it. But... will one day be poor and weak; no longer will a high tree be able to grow from it." That poor soil is the Last Man—amongst whom there is "no herdsman and one herd" because "everyone wants the same thing; everyone is the same." He has barely finished his account when "the shouting and mirth of the crowd interrupted him. 'Give us this Last Man, O Zarathustra'—so they cried—'make us into this Last Man, O Zarathustra! You can have the Superman!'"[85]

The move made by the crowd is one I have elsewhere termed "reading like a loser"—interpreting the possibilities offered by the text to one's own disadvantage.[86] This is not a matter of espousing or denying specific values, or of having a positive or negative valuation of anything, including the value of valuation or even the value of devaluation; it is merely a matter of assuming a trajectory. In this case, presented with the alternatives of paths that lead toward the Superman and the animal, the latter "a laughing stock, or a painful embarrassment," the crowd turns away from the Superman toward the animal.

What does that turn represent? The Superman and the Last Man do not constitute concurrent alternatives within Nietzsche's ecology of value in that they represent mutually incompatible possibilities. (An ecology that sustained the Superman could not accommodate the Last Man, and vice versa.) Rather, they represent a choice between trajectories. This choice is similar to, but not the same as, that represented by Nietzsche's challenge, "Either abolish your reverences or—*yourselves*," which presented to the Christian the alternatives of either an active nihilism or a more consistent passive nihilism of the kind represented by Buddhism. However, reading like a loser is not a counterethic like that of Christianity, nor a will to destruction like that of the Buddhist. Neither value-positing nor annihilationist, it is a failure beyond death, a staying alive in order to grow weaker.

In making this choice, the reader also makes a move within Nietzsche's economy. The object of the choice does not define the move; it is rather the trajectory embodied by making one choice rather than the other, the orientation of the self within the individual movements of ascent and descent that make up the economy of value. For Nietzsche, to read like a loser is to become one. Zarathustra tells the crowd: "The Superman is the meaning of the earth. Let your will say: The Superman *shall* be the meaning of the earth!" They reply, "Give us this Last Man...Make us into this Last Man." It is the response of the crowd that creates the Last Man, a race "as inexterminable as the flea." By opting for a descending trajectory independent of the ascending trajectory of the Superman, the crowd opts for preemptive defeat, a failure that creates losers without victors: surplus failures.

The herd, a sum of zeroes, is not necessarily the most negative ecology possible. An ecology that ensures that everyone is a zero prevents the emergence of both the exceptionally strong and the exceptionally weak: "The instinct of the herd considers the middle and the mean as the highest and most valuable…[and] feels the exception whether it be below or above it, as something opposed and harmful to it."[87] The herd therefore seeks to defend itself on both sides: against those above and "against those who have degenerated from it (criminals, etc.)."[88]

As Nietzsche here implies, reading like a loser does not necessarily reach its limit with the herd. The social constituency of the herd is variously defined in terms of species (the cow, the lamb, the "little good-natured sheep"); in terms of social position (the "people," the "slaves," the "plebians"); or in terms of health ("those who are from the outset victims, downtrodden, broken—they are the ones, the *weakest* are the ones who most undermine life").[89] In every case these are relative positions—relative to predator animals, the aristocracy, or the healthy—though in some cases they are purely relative (predator/prey, and master/slave) and in others comparative (healthy/sick).[90]

Egalitarianism ends direct exploitation by bringing the minority of exploiters down to the level of the exploited; it puts an end to purely relative inequality but not to comparative inequality. Even without exploitation there is still a difference between the healthy and the sick or, as Nietzsche puts it in *Genealogy*, between "the bell with a full tone" and "the one which is cracked and out of tune." Like William Cowper's "stricken deer, that left the herd," the loser may assume a trajectory of failure relative to the herd itself. This is not necessarily through direct exploitation by the herd: a failure to keep up, an inability to maintain parity with one's equals, is enough for a gap to open up. Within an unequal society, reading like a loser increases equality. Within an equal society, reading like a loser is always undermining egalitarianism, threatening to defeat equality through simple failure. As such, it is the route not only to equality but also beyond it, to the extraegalitarian, to the less than zero.

Nietzsche notes that "[t]here is a point in the history of society when it becomes so pathologically soft and tender that among other things it sides even with those who harm it, criminals, and does this quite seriously and honestly."[91] Reading like a loser takes society to just this point (and beyond), continually devaluing the herd by slowing it to a pace slower than that of the weakest member acknowledged to remain within it. If egalitarianism produces (and is produced by) a society that no longer has the strength to exploit, extraegalitarianism produces a society in which no one is left behind or, as Nietzsche puts it, "a society that no longer has the strength to *excrete*."[92]

A society that cannot excrete will poison itself, for it is a society in which there is a negative ecology of value, a society that generates nihilism. Could this be what a society is for? And if so, what sort of nihilism is this, and how does it differ from that which Nietzsche thinks he has completed?

For Nietzsche, the negation of value requires valuation, if only in the form of devaluation. In order for there to be (de)valuation there must be valuers and social arrangements that permit (de)valuation to take place. Nihilism, in the form of the individual negation of value, may have no limit in terms of the values that may be negated, but it does have a limit in terms of the ecology that will sustain (de)valuation. Nihilism is individual and its limit is social.

Assuming that nihilism requires nihilists, Nietzsche does not distinguish a society that generates nihilists from a society that generates nihilism. It is this that allows him to uncouple the ecology of nihilism from the ecology of value and argue that an ecology of nihilism is ultimately a positive one insofar as it must sustain the most perfect nihilists possible. But Nietzsche also allows us to see beyond this argument. If nihilism is the devaluation of value, where value is merely the ecology that permits devaluation, value is devalued not by a valuer devaluing the value in question, but by a reduction in the overall capacity for valuation or devaluation to take place.

Although produced by individual failure, such nihilism is social rather than individual in form, in that what is specifically nihilistic about it is its negative impact on the ecology of (de)valuation. Paradoxically, therefore, this is an ecology in which skepticism defines rather than extends the scope of nihilism. For Nietzsche, individual skepticism reaches its limit in the ecology needed to maintain it; failure, which undermines that ecology, is also potentially limitless. But not all failure is nihilistic; it furthers the history of nihilism only insofar as it undermines whatever is currently of value—in this case, the ecology of extreme skepticism itself.

Even so, on this account, the desert can always spread a little further. In the process, it leaves some of nihilism's characteristic features behind, for this is a nihilism that spreads without nihilists, a nihilism that cannot articulate its own skepticism.

Nietzsche's question can now be restated: could one sacrifice the development of mankind to help a lower species than man come into existence? Perhaps. In *Zarathustra*, the Voluntary Beggar says that "[i]f we do not alter and become as cows, we shall not enter into the kingdom of heaven."[93] Seeking to learn from them, he had been talking to the cows for half the morning, and they were "just about to reply" when Zarathustra's arrival interrupted the conversation.

We can discover what they might have said from an earlier passage in the *Untimely Meditations*:

> Consider the cattle, grazing as they pass you by....This is a hard sight for man to see, for…a life neither bored nor painful, is precisely what he wants, yet he cannot have it for he refuses to be like an animal. A human being may well ask an animal: "Why do you not speak to me of your happiness but only stand and gaze at me?" The animal would like to answer, and say: "[T]he reason is I always forget what I was going to say," but then he forgot this answer too, and stayed silent: so that the human being was left wondering.[94]

Endnotes

1 See Michael Allen Gillespie, *Nihilism Before Nietzsche* (Chicago, 1995).

2 Friedrich Nietzsche, *The Gay Science*, trans. Walter Kaufmann (New York, 1974), 347; hereafter GS. (Unless otherwise indicated, references to Nietzsche's works are to section numbers rather than pages). For the political background to Nietzsche's thought see Domenico Losurdo's magisterial *Nietzsche, il ribelle aristocratico* (Turin, 2004).

3 *New York Times*, April 24, 1881.

4 Jean Richepin, *Cauchemars* (Paris, 1892), p. 59 (my translation). (The story "La Comtesse Satan" is occasionally to be found in English translation, wrongly attributed to Guy de Maupassant.)

5 Friedrich Nietzsche, *Writings from the Late Notebooks*, trans. Kate Sturge (Cambridge, 2003), 2.127; hereafter LN. (Friedrich Nietzsche, *The Will to Power*, trans. Walter Kaufmann and R. J. Hollingdale [New York, 1967], 1; hereafter WP). Wherever possible, references to Nietzsche's notebooks include both the notebook and section number in the standard Colli-Montinari edition (also used in LN) and the section number in WP. The immediate source is given first, followed by the corresponding reference in parentheses. LN indicates that the note is translated in *Late Notebooks*, otherwise references are to Giorgio Colli and Mazzino Montinari, eds., *Friedrich Nietzsche, Sämtliche Werke, Kritische Gesamtausgabe*, 30 vols. (Berlin, 1967–78), vol. 8, unless another volume is specified.

6 Friedrich Nietzsche, *On the Genealogy of Morals*, trans. Douglas Smith (Oxford, 1996), preface, 5 (translation modified); hereafter GM.

7 LN, 2.127 (WP, 1).

8 LN, 5.71.1 (WP, 4).

9 LN, 2.114 (WP, 845).

10 GS, 346.

11 WP, 28 (10.42).

12 WP, preface, 4 (11.411).

13 WP, 28 (10.42).

14 LN, 9.35 (WP, 13).

15 LN, 9.35 (WP, 23).

16 WP, 585 (9.60).

17 LN, 10.17 (WP, 866).

18 Other attempts to systematize the varieties of nihilism found in Nietzsche's thought include Gilles Deleuze, *Nietzsche and Philosophy*, trans. Hugh Tomlinson (London, 1983), p. 139 ff.; Alan White, "Nietzschean Nihilism: A Typology," *International Studies in Philosophy* 19 (1987): pp.

29–44; Elisabeth Kuhn, *Friedrich Nietzsches Philosophie des europäischen Nihilismus* (Berlin, 1992), and Bernard Reginster, *The Affirmation of Life* (Cambridge, MA, 2006).

[19] Friedrich Nietzsche, *Ecce Homo*, trans. R. J. Hollingdale (Harmondsworth, 1979), p. 79 (hereafter EH); 11.280.

[20] LN, 5.71.10,13 (WP, 55).

[21] LN, 5.71.3–4 (WP, 114 and 55).

[22] LN, 2.127 (WP, 1).

[23] LN, 14.123 (WP, 685).

[24] GS, 347.

[25] Friedrich Nietzsche, *The Birth of Tragedy*, trans. Walter Kaufmann (New York, 1967), 7; see F. Max Müller, *Selected Essays* (London, 1881).

[26] Friedrich Nietzsche, *The Anti-Christ*, trans. R. J. Hollingdale (Harmondsworth, 1968), 20; hereafter AC.

[27] WP, 585 (9.60).

[28] AC, 22.

[29] WP, 64 (translation modified) (9.82).

[30] LN, 9.35 (WP, 13).

[31] Friedrich Nietzsche, *Beyond Good and Evil*, trans. Walter Kaufmann (New York, 1966), 202; hereafter BGE.

[32] LN, 2.127 (WP, 1).

[33] WP, 458 (14.107).

[34] LN, 5.71.12 (WP, 55).

[35] LN, 5.71.6 (WP, 55).

[36] BGE, 56.

[37] LN, 5.71.14 (WP, 55).

[38] LN, 9.35 (WP, 23).

[39] WP, 585 (9.60).

[40] WP, 675 (LN, 11.96); WP, 13 (LN, 9.35).

[41] Keith Ansell Pearson, "Nietzsche and Nihilism," http://www.newstatesman.com/blogs/the-faith-column/2007/11/sense-nietzsche-nihilism-life, posted November 8, 2007; see also, Gianni Vattimo, *Nihilism and Emancipation*, trans. Santiago Zabala (New York, 2004), p. 54.

[42] LN, 5.71.3, 5, 6 (WP, 114 and 55).

[43] LN, 10.94 (WP, 749).

[44] GM, preface, 5; 2.24; preface, 3.

45 WP, 112 (LN, 10.22).

46 WP, 1041 (16.32).

47 WP, 2 (LN, 9.35).

48 WP, 675 and 55 (LN, 11.96 and 5.71.10).

49 WP, 708 (LN, 11.72).

50 WP, 711 (LN, 11.74).

51 WP, 53 (14.40).

52 LN, 11.72 (WP, 708).

53 WP, 339 (LN, 11.226).

54 EH, p. 129.

55 EH, p. 130.

56 WP, 315 (9.173).

57 WP, 660 (LN 2.76).

58 EH, p. 129 (translation modified).

59 LN, 9.44 (WP, 27).

60 WP, 37 (9.107).

61 LN, 5.71.14 (WP 55).

62 LN 5.71.12 (WP 55).

63 LN, 5.64 (WP 657).

64 LN, 7.48.

65 WP, 56 (11.150).

66 WP, 957 (LN 37.8).

67 WP, 660 (LN 2.76).

68 WP, 859 (7.6 [p. 289]).

69 LN, 10.17 (WP, 866).

70 LN, 11.73 (translation modified) (WP, 715).

71 LN, 5.61 (translation modified).

72 LN, 11.73 (WP 715).

73 AC, 55; GS, 358.

74 WP, 960 (2 57).

75 Like the Prussian officer corps, or the Jesuits (WP, 796; LN, 2.114).

76 GM, 2.17 (translation modified); WP, 960 (LN, 2.57).

77 WP, 32 (6.25).

78 BGE, 202.

79 WP, 125 (vol. 7, 37.11).

80 BGE, 203.

81 WP, 872 (vol. 7, 25.343).

82 For example, a society in which half the lower types were exploited would contain less value than one in which all were exploited, and a society in which only a quarter were exploited still less, even if the actual numbers of those exploited remained the same.

83 WP, 713 (14.8).

84 BGE, 203.

85 Friedrich Nietzsche, *Thus Spoke Zarathustra*, trans. R. J. Hollingdale (Harmondsworth, 1961), 46–77 (translation modified).

86 Malcolm Bull, "Where Is the Anti-Nietzsche," *New Left Review* 3 (2000): pp. 121–45.

87 WP, 280 (10.39).

88 WP, 285 (vol. 7, 27.17).

89 BGE, 203; GM, 1.9 and 3.14.

90 Although Nietzsche believes that relative positions should naturally reflect comparative ones, he acknowledges that they do not necessarily map over. The sick can get the better of the healthy—which is exactly what happened in "the slave revolt in morals," as a result of which "the people" have won and "the 'masters' are done away with" (GM, 1.9).

91 BGE, 201.

92 WP, 50 (16.53).

93 Nietzsche, *Zarathustra*, p. 280.

94 Friedrich Nietzsche, *Untimely Meditations*, trans. R. J. Hollingdale (Cambridge, 1983), pp. 60–61.

T. J. Clark

My Unknown Friends: A Response to Malcolm Bull

In December 2007 Malcolm Bull gave two seminars at the Townsend Center under the title "Social Nihilism." His essay in this volume is drawn from the material presented there. Henry Staten, Judith Butler, and I were commentators. What follows is the text of my short reply to his first paper.

I INVITED MALCOLM BULL to Berkeley for many reasons, but perhaps chief among them was the fact that I have yet to recover from reading an essay he published eight years ago in _New Left Review_ entitled "Where Is the Anti-Nietzsche?" The essay still puts me on the spot, I find; me and those many others—those left-Nietzscheans, for want of a better word—who have looked to Nietzsche for guidance over the past century. The paper Bull has just presented takes the argument of the essay into new territory, and the stakes of an opposition to Nietzsche and Nietzscheanism of any stripe are clarified. Escape from Nietzsche's orbit, Malcolm Bull believes, will come only from a root-and-branch rejection of Nietzsche's anthropology. And this will entail revisiting, and reconstructing, the Marx of the 1844 manuscripts, and putting the very notion of "species-being" in question. It will involve, in a word, redrawing the line between the human and the animal.

Malcolm Bull is pursuing a great thought-experiment. I have

the sense that many will feel obliged to react to his challenge in the coming years. But I confess that I am still assimilating the latest stages in his argument, and I hope he will forgive me if I use this occasion to go back to the grounds of his first attack, in the *NLR* essay, and try to situate myself in relation to that. For as I say, no other critique of Nietzsche, and there have been many, conjures up the actual reader of *Daybreak* and *The Case of Wagner* so unnervingly.

"In reading Nietzsche," Bull writes,

> our exercise of the will to power is actually rewarded with the experience of power. It is possible to see this happen even in a single sentence. Take Nietzsche's boast in *Ecce Homo*, "I am not a man I am dynamite." Reading these words, who has not felt the sudden thrill of something explosive within themselves; or, at the very least, emboldened by Nietzsche's daring, allowed themselves to feel a little more expansive than usual. This, after all, is the way we usually read. Even though Nietzsche is attributing the explosive power to himself, not to us, we instantly appropriate it for ourselves.[1]

Or, to sum up the diagnosis in an aphorism: "Reading Nietzsche successfully means reading for victory, reading so that we identify ourselves with the goals of the author." What Bull wants, by contrast—and what he thinks we left-Nietzscheans lack—is a way of reading the texts of the 1880s that truly disidentifies from Nietzsche's predatory and aristocratic view of existence and the value it puts on the exceptional individual. "Reading like a loser" is his phrase for this move: reading, consistently and relentlessly, from the position of the ill-formed, the uncreative, the discarded, the undistinguished, the philistine, the lowest common denominator of the human—or even from that of the less-than-human, the subhuman, the merely mortal.

It is, I think, an astonishing call to arms (or to disarm), and a response to it has no alternative but to be basic. Because Bull's critique goes to the root of our wishes and procedures as readers, it obliges me to start—or try to start—from the same place. What follows is a brief attempt to say why one reader (a reader who feels no stirring of excitement, by the way, at Nietzsche's pronouncements on dynamite) goes on turning back to *The Genealogy of Morals* and *The Will to Power*.

What, in other words, remains indispensable in Nietzsche, even after Bull's critique? And indispensable specifically for a "left"— for a project of opposition to the present order of things (and to the present forms of opposition to those things)? What is it that left-Nietzscheans have thought they could take advantage of, in the thought of such an obviously reactionary thinker?

I apologize for the nervous scare-quotes around the word "left," and from now on will drop them. But of course they speak to something real. And it follows that there is a brief piece of historical scene-setting necessary before I can answer the questions just posed. I do not think my answers will make much sense unless I spell out what sort of moment, historically, the left seems to me to be living through. I would say that it is something like the moment after Waterloo in Europe—the moment of Restoration, of apparent world-historical immobility (though vigorous re-constellation of the productive forces) in the interim between 1815 and 1830 or 1840. In terms of the overall project of Enlightenment, this was a moment between paradigms. The long arc of rational and philosophical critique—the arc from Hobbes to Descartes to Diderot to Jefferson to Kant—had ended. Looking back with hindsight, we can see that beneath the polished surface of Restoration the elements of a new vision of human possibility were assembling— peculiar mutations of utilitarianism and political economy, the speculations of Saint-Simon, Fourier's counterfactuals, the intellectual energies of the Young Hegelians. But it was, at the time (in the shadow of Metternich, Ingres, the later Coleridge), extremely hard to see these elements for what they were, let alone as capable of coalescing into a new form of opposition—a new conception of what it was that had to be opposed, and a new intuition of the standpoint from which opposition might be possible. This is the way the Restoration resembles our own time: in its sense that a previous language and set of presuppositions for emancipation had run into the sands, and its realistic uncertainty as to whether the elements of a new language were to be found at all, in the general spectacle of frozen politics, ruthless economy, and enthusiasm (as always) for the new.

The question for the left at such moments is how *deep* does its reconstruction of the project of Enlightenment have to go? "How far down?" Some of us think, "Seven levels of the world." And some of us think that in the process of reconstruction we shall have to take the risk of the kinds of contamination (the reading for victory) that Bull describes so eloquently. Nietzsche, that is, comes up as a resource for the left only at the moment of the left's historical defeat—only when events oblige us to ask ourselves what it was, in our previous failed stagings of transfiguration, that led to the present debacle. No doubt the various movements of opposition to the new world order were defeated by real opponents, whose actual power and cruelty were time and again decisive; but equally obviously, the movements defeated themselves and stood, in the end, too close to their opponents' worldview.

How does Nietzsche help us consider that self-defeat, and suggest the elements for a way beyond it? I shall offer four lines of reply. Let me start on the most familiar left-Nietzschean ground. For a tradition that staked so much, over two centuries, on a historical dramaturgy in which tremendous *identities* held center stage—historical class subjects, forces and entities in whom the becoming of Enlightenment was believed to take on flesh—it still matters enormously that Nietzsche gives us another way of conceiving identities in general; and, in particular, the identity Nietzsche more than once calls that on which the whole architecture of Being rests: the "subject," the "individual." That this aspect of left-Nietzscheanism can easily morph into a fantasy of a world from which identities have disappeared outright, or been made wholly contingent on some ubiquitous virtualizing apparatus, I do not dispute. But this is the fantasists' problem, not Nietzsche's. His is a world of constituted identities, needless to say, stubborn and inventive in the pursuit of self-perpetuation; but a world in which identities come and go, always made out of multiplicity, always reaching toward an otherness, a nonidentity, that *will* be made part of the oneness, but whose resistance, whose opacity, is what the oneness most needs.[2] I cannot, in other words, imagine a future left politics that would not be, centrally, a nonidentity politics. Therefore Nietzsche's thinking of the problem, incomplete as it is, cannot be avoided.

The same goes for Nietzsche's critique of an ethics and politics based on *ressentiment*. This is a dauntingly complex topic (Nietzsche's ambivalence on the issue in *The Genealogy of Morals*, conceptually and rhetorically, goes on defying paraphrase), and I shall do no more than point to the questions wrapped up in it. Clearly it is the case that Nietzsche recoiled from a moment he imagined in human history at which the powerless and downtrodden took the Yes and No of valuation in their hands—symbolically, institutionally—and made power evil and powerlessness good. He recoiled for many reasons, but somewhere at the heart of them was a conviction of the futility (the false humility) of a picture of the political and ethical world premised on negation—on a notion of justice that had no positive content, he believed, or far too little, and that turned on rancor at the powers and privileges of others. Nietzsche's thought on this issue, as I say, leads off in various dialectical directions. He is very far from thinking the moment of *ressentiment*—the invention of slave morality—merely empty and unproductive. On the contrary: he knows it deepens man and carves out a specific space of interiority: it makes man more "interesting"; it may even be the moment that gives rise to the idea—the strange idea—of beauty.[3] *Ressentiment* is a productive negation. Nietzsche admires and fears it; but above all he does not believe it can form the basis of a sustainable, defensible view of the world—a proposal of the good life, an imaginative affirming of certain purposes and possibilities and a true (equally imaginative) denial of others.

The kernel of this critique of *ressentiment* seems to me to speak directly to the tragedy of twentieth-century socialisms. I cannot see how we shall confront the full measure of that tragedy without Nietzsche in mind. The question of *ressentiment* is intertwined with that of otherworldliness, specifically with Christianity, but also with a more pervasive will to avoid or negate the brute fact of existence—the fact that this material world is the only one we shall ever have. I am no defender of Nietzsche's often vicious and ridiculous picture of the socialism and anarchism of his time—of course it is powered by ignorance and fear. But one thing he does get right, and it is a "one thing" that the history of the last hundred years (and the present recrudescence of wars of religion) makes central to any reconstruction of politics. The visions, idioms, and eschatologies of the left are contaminated with the Christianity from which they arose. Otherworldiness—utopia, apocalyptic futurity, the communion of class saints, the priesthood of the Party—goes on singing its life-denying song at the heart of revolution. And what a truly worldly politics of the left would look like—a politics without illusions, without the future in its bones, truly and properly pessimistic, and *therefore* maximalist in its demands—is a question that can only be broached, I believe, with Nietzsche's help. I agree profoundly with Bull—it strikes me as ultimately what drives his whole thought-experiment—that a new form of worldliness is the order of the day. ("Day" is a metaphor, which implies nothing about the pace and pain of reconstruction.)

Another way of putting this would be to say that Nietzsche lets us discriminate between the kinds of pessimism we need and those we may need to reject—between any variant of Christian hopelessness, sinfulness, and immutable nature and what he went on calling the pessimism of strength. Here is a point where Bull's reading of Nietzsche and mine specifically diverge. For Bull, if I follow him rightly, the negative or *un*assertive moment of power in Nietzsche is inessential—or certainly not essential to the action and self-understanding of his *powerful*, his band of pitiless predators. I'm not so sure. Power, for Nietzsche, is consciousness of limits—of what in the human and natural world is irremediable, unredeemable. It is a consciousness that does not transpose such recognition into the key of catastrophe or Fall. Power (or the power Nietzsche posits as a value) is the ability *not* to dream the other into a form in which otherness is "taken up" into a fused collectivity or a future always about to arrive. Nietzsche, dare I say it, has his own view of moderation in politics. Bull and I both regard the elaborate note Nietzsche made on 10 June 1887 as one of his key statements. Bull quotes one of its high generalizing moments: "There is nothing to life that has value, except the degree of power—assuming that life itself is the will to power."[4] Fair enough; though Nietzsche being Nietzsche, this is far from his last word on the source of value in human affairs. (Compare *Will to Power* section 13, from a notebook kept over the same months: "This too is merely nihilism....It places the value of things precisely in the lack of any reality corresponding to these values and in their being merely a symptom of strength on the part of the value-positers, a simplification on the part of life.") Suppose, however, we stay with the 10th of June. The main drift of the last two pages of that remarkable exposé is political and predictive. The subject, as usual, is the end of the active moral order of Christendom, and the crisis of self-understanding that nihilism— "this self-destruction of the underprivileged"—represents. It *is* self-destruction, because it puts paid to the idea that each individual, the underprivileged included, has "a metaphysical value" and awaits acknowledgment in some final order of things. But out of the ongoing realization that this consolation for misery is untrue will come—Nietzsche is fully aware that it will come slowly, over centuries, and that men will struggle desperately to reinvent otherworldliness, just because the world *is* intolerable—"a crisis that...purifies, that...pushes together related elements to perish of each other, that...assigns common tasks to men who have opposite ways of thinking...[o]f course, outside every existing social order."

There follows an interesting move. "Who will prove to be the strongest in the course of this?" Nietzsche asks. "The most moderate; those who do not *require* any extreme articles of faith; those who not only concede but actually love a fair amount of contingency and nonsense; those who can think of man with a considerable reduction of his value without becoming small and weak themselves on that account...human beings who are sure of their power and who represent, with conscious pride, the strength that humanity has [actually] achieved."

We could (and ought to) argue about Nietzsche's emphases here. His is a vision of moderacy like no other.[5] But whatever our disagreements, they will surely be about—and no doubt with—Nietzsche's understanding of a sense of limits to human affairs, a sense of the possible, a pessimism that is also a pragmatism; all of them conceived as emerging from *within* the power—the forms of leadership and "conscious pride"—that lie on the other side of the nihilist's abyss. There is, to borrow Bull's vocabulary for a moment, a negative ecology of the victorious just as much as—maybe more than—of the defeated. Nietzsche calls it the pathos of distance, or the pessimism of strength.

Of course section 55 is a note, a sketch. But in my view it has the makings of an actual (speculative) sociology of politics in the absence of socialism—after "revolution," after the anticipation of the end has ceased. And I guess you will pick up my implication that Bull's alternative to that afterwards—his heroic attempt to put true valuelessness at last in place of pessimism, strong or weak—seems to me, for all its irony and modesty, one more version of the *leap*, the ascesis, the abnegation. It is a beautiful version, tonally strange, ethically invincible. But this very radicality—here is my final thought—may be the problem. Thinking on the left is a hall of mirrors: we know that to our cost. Could it be that this way too a new otherworldliness—another utopia—lies?

Endnotes

1   Malcolm Bull, "Where Is the Anti-Nietzsche," *New Left Review* 3 (May–June 2000): 128, reprinted in this volume.

2   Friedrich Nietzsche, *The Will to Power*, trans. W. Kaufmann and R. J. Hollingdale (New York, 1968), 487, 489, 532, 635, 664–68, 674. (Unless otherwise indicated, references to Nietzsche's works are to section numbers rather than pages).

3   Friedrich Nietzsche, *On the Genealogy of Morality*, trans. Maudemarie Clark and Alan Swensen (Indianapolis, 1998), 1.6, 2.18.

4   Nietzsche, *Will to Power*, 55.

5   Typically, Nietzsche's thought on the subject is entangled with a series of naïve, not to say nauseating, remarks on "rank order" as the most precious fruit of the new movement. But even here he confronts the left with a problem still to be thought through in the left's terms. Suppose we substitute "leadership" for rank, and understand the concept as belonging with workmanship, musicianship, seamanship, craftsmanship—that is, having to do with the mastery of specific skills rather than charismatic (hierarchic) power over others. (Not that "mastery of specific skills" is a notion existing apart from established kinds of interpersonal difference. The "man" lurking at the heart of most of the words I bring on as comparanda reminds us of that.) I presume that we would agree that the left has suffered centrally from the lack of a theory, and a political practice, of leadership so conceived. It has accepted the premises of charisma more or less unthinkingly and veered between lofty rejectionism (leadership as an embarrassment, an atavism, from which the project of Enlightenment must free itself) and reinvention with all the most murderous trappings.

Contributors

MALCOLM BULL is Head of Art History at the Ruskin School of Drawing and Fine Art, University of Oxford, and a Fellow of St. Edmund Hall.

ANTHONY J. CASCARDI is Sidney and Margaret Ancker Professor of Comparative Literature, Rhetoric, and Spanish at the University of California, Berkeley.

T.J. CLARK is George C. and Helen N. Pardee Professor of Modern Art at the University of California, Berkeley.

Lightning Source UK Ltd.
Milton Keynes UK
UKOW02f0312290814

237647UK00023B/445/P